SPOTLIGHT

MAINE HIKING

JACQUELINE TOURVILLE

How to Use This Book

ABOUT THE TRAIL PROFILES

Each hike in this book is listed in a consistent, easy-to-read format to help you choose the ideal hike. From a general overview of the setting to detailed driving directions, the profile will provide all the information you need. Here is a sample profile:

Map number and hike number

Round-trip mileage (unless otherwise noted) and the approximate amount of time needed to complete the hike (actual times can vary widely, especially on longer hikes)

Difficulty and quality ratings

General location of the trail, named by its proximity to the nearest major town or landmark

Symbol indicating that the hike is listed among the author's top picks

1 SOMEWHERE USA HIKE

9.0 mi/5.0 hrs   🏃3 ⛰8

at the mouth of the Somewhere River

BEST (

Each hike in this book begins with a brief overview of its setting. The description typically covers what kind of terrain to expect, what might be seen, and any conditions that may make the hike difficult to navigate. Side trips, such as to waterfalls or panoramic vistas, in addition to ways to combine the trail with others nearby for a longer outing, are also noted here. In many cases, mile-by-mile trail directions are included.

User Groups: This section notes the types of users that are permitted on the trail, including hikers, mountain bikers, horseback riders, and dogs. Wheelchair access is also noted here.

Permits: This section notes whether a permit is required for hiking, or, if the hike spans more than one day, whether one is required for camping. Any fees, such as for parking, day use, or entrance, are also noted here.

Maps: This section provides information on how to obtain detailed trail maps of the hike and its environs. Whenever applicable, names of U.S. Geologic Survey (USGS) topographic maps and national forest maps are also included; contact information for these and other map sources are noted in the Resources section at the back of this book.

Directions: This section provides mile-by-mile driving directions to the trail head from the nearest major town.

Contact: This section provides an address and phone number for each hike. The contact is usually the agency maintaining the trail but may also be a trail club or other organization.

ABOUT THE ICONS

The icons in this book are designed to provide at-a-glance information on the difficulty and quality of each hike.

The **difficulty rating** (rated **1-5** with **1** being the lowest and **5** the highest) is based on the steepness of the trail and how difficult it is to traverse.

The **quality rating** (rated **1-10** with **1** being the lowest and **10** the highest) is based largely on scenic beauty, but also takes into account how crowded the trail is and whether noise of nearby civilization is audible.

ABOUT THE DIFFICULTY RATINGS

Trails rated 1 are very easy and suitable for hikers of all abilities, including young children.

Trails rated 2 are easy-to-moderate and suitable for most hikers, including families with active children 6 and older.

Trails rated 3 are moderately challenging and suitable for reasonably fit adults and older children who are very active.

Trails rated 4 are very challenging and suitable for physically fit hikers who are seeking a workout.

Trails rated 5 are extremely challenging and suitable only for experienced hikers who are in top physical condition.

MAP SYMBOLS

▭▭▭▭	Expressway	(80)	Interstate Freeway	✗	Airfield
·········	Primary Road	(101)	U.S. Highway	✗	Airport
▭▭▭▭	Secondary Road	(21)	State Highway	○	City/Town
▭ ▭ ▭ ▭	Unpaved Road	(66)	County Highway	▲	Mountain
············	Ferry	▓	Lake	▲	Park
▬ ▬ ▬	National Border	⌇	Dry Lake	)⌇	Pass
▬ ▬ ▬	State Border	▱	Seasonal Lake	◉	State Capital

Hiking Tips

HIKING ESSENTIALS

It doesn't require much more than a little wilderness knowledge and a backpack's worth of key items to ensure your day hike in New England is a safe and fun adventure. Here's a list of outdoor essentials.

Water and Food

Like any physical activity, hiking increases your body's fluid needs by a factor of two or more. A good rule of thumb for an all-day hike is two liters of water per person, but even that could leave you mildly dehydrated, so carry a third liter if you can. Dehydration can lead to other—more serious—problems, like heat exhaustion, hypothermia, frostbite, and injury. If you're well hydrated, you will urinate frequently and your urine will be clear. The darker your urine, the greater your level of dehydration. If you feel thirsty, dehydration has already commenced. In short: Drink a lot.

Streams and brooks run everywhere in New England. If you're out for more than a day in the backcountry, finding water is rarely a problem (except on ridge tops and summits). But microscopic organisms *Giardia lamblia* and *Cryptosporidium* are common in backcountry water sources and can cause a litany of terrible gastrointestinal problems in humans. Assume you should always treat water from backcountry sources, whether by using a filter or iodine tablets, boiling, or another proven method to eliminate giardiasis and other harmful bacteria. Day-hikers will usually find it more convenient to simply carry enough water from home for the hike.

Similarly, your body consumes a phenomenal amount of calories walking up and down a mountain. Feed it frequently. Carbohydrate-rich foods such as bread, chocolate, dried fruit, fig bars, snack bars, fresh vegetables, and energy bars are all good sources for a quick burst of energy. Fats contain about twice the calories per pound than carbs or protein, and provide the slow-burning fuel that keeps you going all day and keeps you warm through the night if you're sleeping outside; sate your need for fats by eating cheese, chocolate, canned meats or fish, pepperoni, sausage, or nuts.

On hot days, "refrigerate" your water and perishables such as cheese and chocolate: Fill a water bottle (the collapsible kind works best) with very cold water, and ice cubes if possible. Wrap it and your perishables in a thick, insulating fleece and bury it inside your pack. Or the night before, fill a water bottle halfway and freeze it, then fill the remainder with water in the morning before you leave for the hike.

Trail Maps

A map of the park, preserve, or public land you are visiting is essential. Even if you have hiked a trail a hundred times, carry a map. Unexpected trail closures, an injury requiring a shorter route, bad weather, or an animal encounter can all result in a sudden change of plans that require map assistance. Some may believe a GPS device takes the place of a map, but this isn't always true. If you get lost, a detailed trail map showing lakes, rivers, ridge lines, trail junctions, and other landmarks is still the most reliable way to get back on trail.

Many land agencies provide free paper maps at the trailhead, though be aware that some state parks and land agencies are much more vigilant about restocking than others.

GLOBAL POSITIONING SYSTEM (GPS) DEVICES

Working with a system of orbiting satellites, GPS receivers are able to accurately pinpoint your position, elevation, and time anywhere on the face of the earth. Out on the trail, GPS devices can help you navigate from point to point, indicating bearings and the distance remaining to reach your destination. It can also help should you become lost.

Despite these advances, GPS technology is not a replacement for the old standby of a compass and paper topographical map. GPS units are not yet able to provide an adequately detailed view of the surrounding landscape, batteries typically wear out in less than a day, and some landscape conditions can interfere with signal strength. Still, when used in concert with topographical maps, GPS is an extremely useful addition to your navigational toolbox.

Every hike in this book lists GPS coordinates for the hike's trailhead. Use these for better road navigation on the drive to your destination. Inputting the trailhead GPS coordinates before leaving on your hike will also help you retrace your steps if you become lost.

Check the agency's website to see if maps can be printed out beforehand or call to request a map be sent to you. For hikers along the Appalachian Trail, numerous trail maps are available. The best—and most complete—maps are published by the Appalachian Mountain Club and the Appalachian Trail Conservancy.

BLAZES AND CAIRNS
New England's forests abound with blazes—slashes of paint on trees used to mark trails. Sometimes the color of blazes seems random and unrelated to other trails in the same area, but most major trails and trail systems are blazed consistently. The Appalachian Trail (AT) bears white blazes for its entire length, including its 734 miles through five New England states. Most side trails connecting to the AT are blue-blazed. Vermont's 270-mile Long Trail, which coincides with the AT for more than 100 miles, is also blazed in white. Connecticut's Blue Trails system of hiking paths scattered across the state is, as the name suggests, marked entirely with blue blazes.

Although not all trails are well blazed, popular and well-maintained trails usually are—you'll see a colored slash of paint at frequent intervals at about eye level on tree trunks. Double slashes are sometimes used to indicate a sharp turn in the trail. Trails are blazed in both directions, so whenever you suspect you may have lost the trail, turn around to see whether you can find a blaze facing in the opposite direction; if so, you'll know you're still on the trail.

Above tree line, trails may be marked either with blazes painted on rock or with cairns, which are piles of stones constructed at regular intervals. In the rocky terrain on the upper slopes of New England's highest peaks, care may be needed to discern artificially constructed cairns from the landscape surrounding them, but the cairns in rocky areas are usually built higher and are obviously constructed by people.

Extra Clothing
At lower elevations amid the protection of trees or on a warm day, you may elect to bring no extra clothing for an hour-long outing, or no more than a light jacket for a few hours

or more. The exception to this is in the Seacoast region, where hikes are more exposed to cool wind. But higher elevations, especially above tree line, get much colder than the valleys—about three degrees Fahrenheit per thousand feet—and winds can grow much stronger. Many a White Mountains hiker has departed from a valley basking in summerlike weather and reached a summit wracked by wintry winds and lying under a carpet of fresh snow, even during the summer months.

Insulating layers, a jacket that protects against wind and precipitation, a warm hat, gloves, a rain poncho, and extra socks are always a good idea to bring along when out on a long hike, especially when scaling New England's highest peaks. Look for wool blends or the new breed of high tech synthetics, fabrics that wick moisture from your skin and keep you dry. Even on a shorter trek, stowing a jacket, hat, and extra pair of socks in your backpack is always a good idea.

Flashlight

Carrying a flashlight in your pack is a must, even when your hike is planned to end well before dusk. Emergencies happen, and being stuck on the trail after dark without a flashlight only compounds the situation. Plus, if you have ever been in New England right before a thunderstorm, you know fast moving cloud cover can turn the landscape pitch dark in seconds. Micro flashlights with alloy skins, xenon bulbs, and a battery life of eight hours on two AA batteries provide ample illumination and won't add much weight to your pack. Throw in some spare batteries and an extra light—or just pack two flashlights to always be covered. A reliable, compact, and waterproof micro flashlight can typically be purchased for under $20.

Sunscreen and Sunglasses

As you climb to higher elevations, the strength of the sun's ultraviolet rays increases. Applying sunscreen or sunblock to exposed skin and wearing a baseball cap or wide-brimmed hat can easily prevent overexposure to sun. SPF strengths vary, but applying sunscreen at least a half-hour before heading out gives the lotion or spray enough time to take effect. When deciding which sunscreen to buy, look for a fragrance-free formula; strongly scented lotions and sprays may attract mosquitoes. And don't forget your sunglasses. Squinting into the sun for hours on end is not only bad for the delicate skin around your eyes, it's almost a certain way to develop a bad case of eye strain. Look for sunglasses with lenses that provide 100 percent UVA and UVB protection.

First-Aid Kit

It's wise to carry a compact and lightweight first-aid kit for emergencies in the back-country, where an ambulance and hospital are often hours, rather than minutes, away. Prepare any first-aid kit with attention to the type of trip, the destination, and the needs of people hiking (for example, children or persons with medical conditions).

A basic first-aid kit consists of:
- aspirin or an anti-inflammatory
- 4 four-inch-by-four-inch gauze pads
- knife or scissors
- moleskin or Spenco Second Skin (for blisters)
- 1 roll of one-inch athletic tape
- 1 six-inch Ace bandage

- paper and pencil
- safety pins
- SAM splint (a versatile and lightweight splinting device available at many drug stores)
- several alcohol wipes
- several one-inch adhesive bandages
- tube of povidone iodine ointment (for wound care)
- 2 large handkerchiefs
- 2 large gauze pads

Pack everything into a thick, clear plastic resealable bag. And remember, merely carrying a first-aid kit does not make you safe; knowing how to use what's in it does.

HIKING GEAR

Much could be written about how to outfit oneself for hiking in a region like New England, with its significant range of elevations and latitudes, alpine zones, huge seasonal temperature swings, and fairly wet climate.

Don't leave your clothing, gear, and other equipment choices to chance. New England is packed with plenty of friendly, locally owned stores that offer quality, outdoor clothing and footwear options (and knowledgeable staff to help you). Or, take part in the venerable Yankee tradition of the swap meet. Many of New England's mountain clubs hold semi-annual or seasonal meets, giving hikers the irresistible chance to scoop up quality used gear at a very frugal price. Swap meets are also a fun and easy way to meet others in the hiking community.

Clothing

Clothes protect you against the elements and also help to regulate body temperature. What you wear when you go hiking should keep you dry and comfortable, no matter what the weather and season. From underwear to outerwear, pick garments that offer good "breathability." Wool blends and the new breed of synthetic microfibers do a good job at wicking moisture away from the skin. Shirts and pants made from microfiber polyesters are also extra-light and stretchy, allowing for maximum range of movement.

You will also want to dress in layers: underwear, one or more intermediate layers, and, finally, an outer layer. Wearing multiple layers of clothing offers you lots of flexibility for regulating body temperature and exposure. Test your clothing at different temperatures and levels of activity to find out what works best for you.

Rain Gear

Coastal currents smashing up against weather fronts dropping south from Canada give New England its famously fickle weather. Especially in summer, a sunny late morning start to your hike could mean a return trip in a raging rainstorm, often with very little warning time. No matter where you go or how long you expect to be out on the trail, bring along rain gear. It doesn't need to be elaborate: a vinyl foul weather poncho left in its packaging until needed is a compact addition to your pack.

If you do end up getting caught in a thunderstorm or sudden downpour, move away from high ground and tall trees immediately. Take shelter in a low spot, ravine, or thin place in the woods, cover up with your poncho, and wait for the storm to pass. Also,

HIKING GEAR CHECKLIST

Long-distance backpackers need to worry about hauling along camping and cooking equipment, but besides good boots, comfortable clothes, water, food, and a trusty map, it doesn't take much to have all the gear you need for a day hike. Here are some must-haves for your next outing.

IN CASE OF EMERGENCY

Altimeter

Compass

Extra clothes

First-aid kit

Lightweight (or mylar) blanket

Pen/pencil and paper

Swiss army-style knife

Waterproof matches

CREATURE COMFORTS

Binoculars

Bird, wildlife, and tree/flower identification guides

Bug spray/sunscreen

Camera

Face cloths

Fishing pole and fishing license

Picnic supplies

Trekking pole

And, of course, bring along your hiking guide!

look carefully at your surroundings, making sure you are not standing in a dry riverbed or wash while waiting, in case of flash floods.

Being out in rainy weather is also a concern for your feet and legs. Brushing up against wet ferns or low-lying plants can make for uncomfortably damp pant legs and soaked socks and boots. In case you do get stuck in the rain, another good piece of equipment to have on hand is a pair of gaiters, leggings made of Gore-Tex or other water-repellant materials. Gaiters are held in place under each boot with a stirrup and extend over your pants to just below the knee.

Shoes and Socks

The most important piece of gear may be well-fitting, comfortable, supportive shoes or boots. Finding the right footwear requires trying on various models and walking around in them in the store before deciding. Everyone's feet are different, and shoes or boots that feel great on your friend won't necessarily fit you well. Deciding how heavy your footwear should be depends on variables like how often you hike, whether you easily injure feet or ankles, and how much weight you'll carry. My general recommendation is to hike in the most lightweight footwear that you find comfortable and adequately supportive.

There are three basic types of hiking boots. Sneaker-like trail shoes are adequate when you are hiking in a dry climate and on well-established paths. Traditional hiking boots, sometimes called trail hikers or trail boots, are constructed with a higher cut and slightly stiffer sole to provide support on steep inclines and muddy paths. Mountaineering boots are for those who might need to attach crampons for a better grip on glaciers or hard-packed snow on mountain hikes and rock or ice climbing. Mountaineering boots are built with a very stiff sole to give your feet and ankles support and protection as you climb more challenging terrain.

The hiking boot experts at L.L.Bean, New England's premier shopping destination for outdoor gear and equipment, recommend hikers consider the various advantages of fabric-and-leather boots and all-leather boots. Fabric-and-leather boots are lighter and easier to break in, but all-leather boots offer added protection and durability in rigorous terrain, as well as being water resistant and breathable. Quality boots can be found in either style.

HIKING BOOTS

Try boots on at the end of the day when your feet are more swollen and wear the socks you plan to wear on the trail. Boots should feel snug but comfortable, so you can still wiggle your toes. Most hiking boots won't feel as instantly comfortable as sneakers, but they shouldn't pinch, cause hot spots, or constrict circulation. They should fit securely around your ankle and instep. Try walking down an incline at the store. Your feet should not slide forward, nor should your toenails scrape against the front of your boot. If your foot slides forward, the boot could be too wide. If the back of your heel moves around, your boots might not be laced up tight enough.

Once you purchase a pair of boots, break them in slowly with short hikes. Leather boots in particular take a while to break in, so take a couple of two- or three-hour hikes before your big trip or wear them around the house. If you find any sharp pressure points, use leather conditioner to soften the leather.

SOCKS

With exertion, one foot can sweat up to two pints of vapor/fluid per day. That's why wicking technology in hiking socks is so important. Without it, bacteria and fungus can become a problem. The best hiking socks are made from 100 percent wool or a wool blend of at least 50 percent wool. Unlike most synthetic fibers, which have to wait for moisture to condense into a liquid before wicking it away from your skin, wool socks absorb and transfer moisture in its vapor state, before it condenses. When it's hot, this creates a mini air-conditioning unit next to your feet, releasing heat through your socks and boots. And when it's cold, wicking keeps bone-chilling moisture at bay.

Some newer synthetics and synthetic blends are engineered to wick moisture; read the package label carefully and ask the store clerk for recommendations. The one fiber to stay away from is cotton, which absorbs water and perspiration and holds it next to your skin. If you are hiking with wet feet and the temperature drops below freezing, you risk getting frostbite. A good sock system and hiking boots reduce that possibility.

For comfort and good circulation, look for socks that won't bind your feet and avoid those made with excessive stitching or a scratchy knit that could lead to chafing. Terry woven socks are a good pick to distribute pressure and support your natural posture. And thicker isn't always better. Depending on the fit of your boots and the climate you'll be hiking in, a medium-weight wool sock that fits to mid-calf is often your best bet.

FOOTCARE

At an Appalachian Mountain Club hiking seminar, one instructor wisely noted that, besides the brain, "Your feet are the most important part of your body." Hurt any other

THE APPALACHIAN TRAIL

Perhaps the most famous hiking trail in the world, the Appalachian Trail (AT) runs 2,174 miles from Springer Mountain in Georgia to Mount Katahdin in Maine, along the spine of the Appalachian Mountains in 14 states. About 734 miles – or more than one-third – of the AT's length passes through five New England states: Connecticut (52 miles), Massachusetts (90 miles), Vermont (150 miles), New Hampshire (161 miles), and Maine (281 miles). New England boasts some of the AT's most spectacular, best-known, and rugged stretches, including the White Mountains, the southern Green Mountains, the Riga Plateau of Massachusetts and Connecticut, and Maine's Mahoosuc, Saddleback, and Bigelow ranges, 100-mile Wilderness, and Katahdin. A few hundred people hike the entire trail end to end every year, but thousands more take shorter backpacking trips and day hikes somewhere along the AT.

Maintained by hiking clubs that assume responsibility for different sections of the AT, the trail is well marked with signs and white blazes on trees and rocks above tree line. Shelters and campsites are spaced out along the AT so that backpackers have choices of where to spend each night. But those shelters can fill up during the busy season of summer and early fall, especially on weekends. The prime hiking season for the AT in New England depends on elevation and latitude, but generally, that season runs May-October in southern New England and mid-June-early October at higher elevations in northern New England.

body part and we might conceivably still make it home under our own power. Hurt our feet, and we're in trouble.

Take care of your feet. Wear clean socks that wick moisture from your skin while staying dry. Make sure your shoes or boots fit properly, are laced properly, and are broken in if they require it. Wear the appropriate footwear for the type of hiking you plan to do. If you anticipate your socks getting wet from perspiration or water, bring extra socks; on a multiday trip, have dry socks for each day, or at least change socks every other day. On hot days, roll your socks down over your boot tops to create what shoe manufacturers call "the chimney effect," cooling your feet by forcing air into your boots as you walk.

On longer treks, whenever you stop for a short rest on the trail—even if only for 5 or 10 minutes—sit down, pull off your boots and socks, and let them and your feet dry out. When backpacking, wash your feet at the end of the day. If you feel any hot spots developing, intervene before they progress into blisters. A slightly red or tender hot spot can be protected from developing into a blister with an adhesive bandage, tape, or a square of moleskin.

If a blister has formed, clean the area around it thoroughly to avoid infection. Sterilize a needle or knife in a flame, then pop and drain the blister to promote faster healing. Put an antiseptic ointment on the blister. Cut a piece of moleskin or Second Skin (both of which have a soft side and a sticky side with a peel-off backing) large enough to overlap the blistered area. Cut a hole as large as the blister out of the center of the moleskin, then place the moleskin over the blister so that the blister is visible through the hole. If done properly, you should be able to walk without aggravating the blister.

Backpack

When just out for the day, a roomy backpack will do to hold your belongings; toting an over-sized metal frame pack is not necessary unless you plan on camping overnight and need to bring along camp stove, bed roll, tent, and other extra gear. Shoulder straps should be foam padded for comfort. Look for backpacks made of water-resistant nylon. And just like clothes or shoes, try the pack on to make sure it has the fit you want.

Trekking Poles

For hikers who need a little extra physical support, trekking poles or walking sticks relieve feet and legs of tens of thousands of pounds of pressure over the course of an all-day hike. They are particularly useful in helping prevent knee and back pain from rigorous hiking. If you find a good walking stick along your journey, before heading back to your car, leave the stick in an obvious spot for another weary hiker to stumble upon. It warmed the bottom of my heart one day to find at least a dozen walking sticks leaning against a trailhead signpost in Massachusetts, free for anyone to use.

CLIMATE

With New England's biggest peaks in the northern states and its smaller hills and flatlands in the southern states, as well as an ocean moderating the Seacoast climate, this region's fair-weather hikers can find a trail to explore virtually year-round. But the wildly varied character of hiking opportunities here also demands some basic knowledge of and preparation for hitting the trails.

The ocean generally keeps coastal areas a little warmer in winter and cooler in summer than inland areas. Otherwise, any time of year, average temperatures typically grow cooler as you gain elevation or move northward.

New England's prime hiking season stretches for several months from spring through fall, with the season's length depending on the region. In general, summer high temperatures range 60°F–90°F with lows from 50°F to around freezing at higher elevations. Days are often humid in the forests and lower elevations and windy on the mountaintops. July and August see occasional thunderstorms, but July through September is the driest period. August is usually the best month for finding ripe wild blueberries along many trails, especially in northern New England.

September is often the best month for hiking, with dry, comfortable days, cool nights, and few bugs. Fall foliage colors peak anywhere from mid-September or early October in northern New England to early or mid-October in the south; by choosing your destinations well and moving north to south, you can hike through vibrant foliage for three or four successive weekends. The period from mid-October into November offers cool days, cold nights, no bugs, few people, and often little snow.

In the higher peaks of Vermont's Green Mountains, New Hampshire's White Mountains, Maine's northern Appalachians, and along the Appalachian Trail in parts of western Massachusetts and Connecticut, high-elevation snow disappears and alpine wildflowers bloom in late spring; by late October, wintry winds start blowing and snow starts flying (though it can snow above 4,000 feet in any month of the year). Spring trails are muddy at low elevations—some are closed to hiking during the April/May "mud season"—and buried under deep, slushy snow up high, requiring snowshoes. Winter conditions set in by mid-November and can become very severe, even life threatening.

CROSS-COUNTRY SKIING AND SNOWSHOEING

Many hikes in this book are great for cross-country skiing or snowshoeing in winter. But added precaution is needed. Days are short and the temperature may start to plummet by mid-afternoon, so carry the right clothing and don't over-estimate how far you can travel in winter. Depending on snow conditions and your own fitness level and experience with either snowshoes or skis, a winter outing can take much longer than anticipated – and certainly much longer than a trip of similar distance on groomed trails at a cross-country ski resort. Breaking your own trail through fresh snow can also be very exhausting – take turns leading and conserve energy by following the leader's tracks, which also serve as a good return trail.

The proper clothing becomes essential in winter, especially the farther you wander from roads. Wear a base layer that wicks moisture from your skin and dries quickly, middle layers that insulate and do not retain moisture, and a windproof shell that breathes well and is waterproof or water-resistant (the latter type of garment usually breathes much better than something that's completely waterproof). Size boots to fit over a thin, synthetic liner sock and a thicker, heavy-weight synthetic-blend sock. For your hands, often the most versatile system consists of gloves and/or mittens that also can be layered, with an outer layer that's waterproof and windproof and preferably also breathable.

Most importantly, don't overdress: Remove layers if you're getting too hot. Avoid becoming wet with perspiration, which can lead to too much cooling. Drink plenty of fluids and eat snacks frequently to maintain your energy level; feeling tired or cold on a winter outing may be an indication of dehydration or hunger.

As long as you're safe, cautious, and aware, winter is a great time to explore New England's trails. Have fun out there.

Going above the tree line in winter is considered a mountaineering experience by many (though these mountains lack glacier travel and high altitude), so be prepared for harsh cold and strong winds.

The second strongest wind gust ever recorded on Earth was measured on April 12, 1934, at the weather observatory on the summit of New Hampshire's Mount Washington. The gust was clocked at 231 mph. The summit of Mount Washington remains in clouds 60 percent of the time. Its average temperature year-round is 26.5°F; winds average 35 mph and exceed hurricane force (75 mph) on average 104 days a year. Be aware that in the higher peaks of the Whites as well as alpine peaks in Vermont and Maine, weather conditions change rapidly. It is not uncommon to set off from the trailhead in hot, sunny weather only to hit driving rain and hail on the summit.

In the smaller hills and flatlands of central and southern New England, the snow-free hiking season often begins by early spring and lasts into late autumn. Some of these trails are even occasionally free of snow during the winter, or offer opportunities for snowshoeing or cross-country skiing in woods protected from strong winds, with warmer temperatures than you'll find on the bigger peaks up north. Many Seacoast trails, even in Maine, rarely stay snow-covered all winter, though they can get occasional heavy snowfall and be very icy in cold weather. For more information about weather-related trail conditions, refer to the individual hike listings.

SAFETY AND FIRST AID

Few of us would consider hiking a high-risk activity. But like any physical activity, it does pose certain risks, and it's up to us to minimize them. For starters, make sure your physical condition is adequate for your objective—the quickest route to injury is over-extending either your skills or your physical abilities. You wouldn't presume that you could rock climb a 1,000-foot cliff if you've never climbed before; don't assume you're ready for one of New England's hardest hikes if you've never—or not very recently—done anything nearly as difficult.

Build up your fitness level by gradually increasing your workouts and the length of your hikes. Beyond strengthening muscles, you must strengthen the soft connective tissue in joints like knees and ankles that are too easily strained and take weeks or months to heal from injury. Staying active in a variety of activities—hiking, running, bicycling, Nordic skiing—helps develop good overall fitness and decreases the likelihood of an overuse injury. Most importantly, stretch muscles before and after a workout to reduce the chance of injury.

New England's most rugged trails—and even parts of its more moderate paths—can be very rocky and steep. Uneven terrain is often a major contributor to falls resulting in serious, acute injury. Most of us have a fairly reliable self-preservation instinct—and you should trust it. If something strikes you as dangerous or beyond your abilities, don't try it, or simply wait until you think you're ready for it.

An injury far from a road also means it may be hours before the victim reaches a hospital. Basic training in wilderness first aid is beneficial to anyone who frequents the mountains, even recreational hikers. New England happens to have two highly respected sources for such training, and the basic course requires just one weekend. Contact SOLO (Conway, NH, 603/447-6711, www.soloschools.com) or Wilderness Medical Associates (Scarborough, ME, 207/730-7331, www.wildmed.com) for information.

Plants

From fern-choked forest floors to fields filled with wild blueberries, plant life in New England is varied and diverse. And luckily, there are only a few poisonous plant species to be wary of: poison ivy, poison oak, and poison sumac. The three plants contain urushiol, an oil that causes an allergic reaction and rash in humans. According to the American Academy of Dermatology, humans typically come in contact with urushiol by brushing up against or touching the plants, touching an object or animal that has come in contact with the oil, or breathing in urushiol particles if a poison plant is burned in a campfire.

Urushiol penetrates the skin in minutes, but the rash usually takes anywhere from 12 to 72 hours to appear, followed quickly by severe itching, redness, swelling, and even blisters. When the rash develops, streaks or lines often reveal where the plant brushed against the skin. A rash triggered by urushiol does not spread and is not contagious.

Recognizing Poisonous Plants

Hikers best protection against the itchy rash caused by urushiol is learning how to identify the plants that contain the oil.

Poison Ivy: Leaves of three, let them be... Poison ivy grows as vines or low shrubs almost everywhere in New England and true to that famous phrase from summer camp, the plant consists of three pointed leaflets; the middle leaflet has a much longer stalk than the two side ones. Leaflets are reddish when they bud in spring, turn green during the summer, and then become various shades of yellow, orange, or red in the autumn. Small greenish flowers grow in bunches attached to the main stem close to where each leaf joins it. Later in the season, clusters of poisonous berries form. They are whitish, with a waxy look.

Poison Oak: There are two main species of poison oak, but the species commonly found in New England is the Atlantic Poison Oak a vine plant or bush. Poison oak leaves grow in clusters of three leaves; the lobbed appearance of each leaf resembles the white oak. Plants put out berries in spring that are white or yellowish-green in color and leaflets change color with the seasons. Poison oak tends to grow in sandy soils.

Poison Sumac: Though it is one of New England's native tree species, poison sumac is the rarest of the urushiol-containing plants. Sumac can be identified by its row of paired

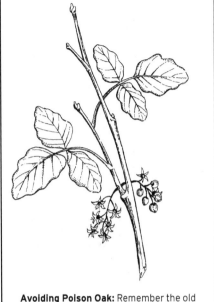

Avoiding Poison Oak: Remember the old Boy Scout saying: "Leaves of three, let them be."

leaflets that contains an additional leaflet at the end. Often the leaves have spots that resemble blotches of black enamel paint. These spots are actually urushiol, which when exposed to air turn brownish-black. Poison sumac tends to grow near wet areas and bogs.

TREATING POISON IVY, POISON OAK, AND POISON SUMAC

When an allergic reaction develops, the skin should be washed well with lukewarm water and soap. All clothing should be laundered, and everything else that may be contaminated with urushiol should be washed thoroughly. Urushiol can remain active for a long time. For mild cases, cool showers and an over-the-counter product that eases itching can be effective. Oatmeal baths and baking-soda mixtures also can soothe the discomfort. When a severe reaction develops contact a dermatologist immediately, or go to an emergency room. Prescription medication may be needed to reduce the swelling and itch.

Insects

Black flies, or mayflies, emerge by late April or early May and pester hikers until late June or early July, while mosquitoes come out in late spring and dissipate (but do not disappear) by midsummer. No-see-ums (tiny biting flies that live up to their name) plague some wooded areas in summer. Of particular concern in recent years has been the small, but growing number of cases of eastern equine encephalitis (EEE) in humans, spread by EEE-infected mosquitoes. It's still very rare, but cases of EEE tend to emerge each year at the end of summer and early fall. Mosquitoes acquire EEE through contact with diseased birds.

LYME DISEASE

Deer ticks are often carriers of the bacteria that causes Lyme disease. Hundreds of cases of the disease – most mild and treatable with antibiotics – are diagnosed in New England each year. The easiest way to avoid tick bites is to wear socks, long pants, and a long-sleeve shirt whenever you hike, and especially when you hike in areas with tall grass and/or large deer populations. Tucking your pant legs into your socks prevents the best protection against the tiny ticks, but never fail to check your skin thoroughly at the end of a hike. Most tick bites cause a sharp sting, but some may go unnoticed.

If you do find a tick, don't panic. Take a pair of tweezers and place them around the tick as close to your skin as possible. Gently pull the tick straight out to avoid parts of it breaking off still attached to the skin. The majority of tick bites are no more of a nuisance than a mosquito or black fly bite. If you do notice a rash spreading out from around the bite within a week of finding the tick, it may be an early sign of Lyme disease. Other symptoms are similar to the flu – headache, fever, muscle soreness, neck stiffness, or nausea – and may appear anywhere from a few days to a week or so after being bitten. If you do notice any symptoms, seek medical help immediately. When caught in its early stages, Lyme disease is easily treated with antibiotics; left untreated, the disease can be debilitating.

You will want to have some kind of bug repellant with you no matter where your hike takes you. (Even the windswept coast isn't free of insects; New England's swarms of black flies first appear on the coast and then move inland.) There is much debate about the health effects of wearing sprays containing the chemical DEET; some may prefer ointments made with essential oils and herbs believed to deter bugs. Or skip the sprays and salves and wear a lightweight jacket made of head-to-waist (or head-to-toe) mosquito netting. These unusual creations are made by Bug Baffler, a New Hampshire-based company, and sold on the web (www.bugbaffler.com).

Wildlife

The remarkable recovery of New England's mountains and forests during the past century from the abuses of the logging industry has spawned a boom in the populations of many wild animals, from increased numbers of black bears and moose to the triumphant return of the bald eagle and peregrine falcon. For the most part, you don't have to worry about your safety in the backcountry when it comes to wildlife encounters. It's typical for hikers to see lots of scat and a traffic jam of prints on the trail without ever actually spotting the animals that left this evidence behind.

Still, a few sensible precautions are in order. If you're camping in the backcountry, know how to hang or store your food properly to keep it from bears and smaller animals like mice, which are more likely to be a problem. You certainly should never approach the region's two largest mammals: moose, which you may see in northern New England, or bear, which you may never see. These creatures are wild and unpredictable, and a moose can weigh several hundred pounds and put the hurt on a much smaller human. The greatest danger posed by moose is that of hitting one while driving on dark back roads at night; hundreds of collisions occur in Maine and New Hampshire every year, often wrecking vehicles and injuring people. At night, drive more slowly than you would during daylight. As one forest ranger warns, "the most dangerous part of hiking in the mountains is the drive to the trailhead."

First Aid
HYPOTHERMIA
In humans and other warm-blooded animals, core body temperature is maintained near a constant level through internal temperature regulation. When the body is over-exposed to cold, however, internal mechanisms may be unable to replenish excessive heat loss. Hypothermia is defined as any body temperature below 95°F (35 °C). Despite its association with winter, hypothermia can occur even when the air temperature is in the 50s. Often the victim has gotten wet or over-exerted himself or herself on the trail. Hypothermia is a leading cause of death in the outdoors.

Symptoms of hypothermia include uncontrollable shivering, weakness, loss of coordination, confusion, cold skin, drowsiness, frost bite, and slowed breathing or heart rate. If a member of your hiking party demonstrates one or more of these symptoms, send a call out for help and take action immediately. Get out of the wind and cold and seek shelter in a warm, dry environment. Help the victim change into windproof, waterproof clothes and wrap up in a blanket, if one is available; start a fire to add extra warmth. Encourage the victim to eat candy, energy bars, and other high-sugar foods to boost energy. Do not offer alcohol, it only makes heat loss worse.

Victims of mild to moderate hypothermia may be suffering from impaired judgment and not be making rational decisions. They might try to resist help; be persistent.

HEAT STROKE
Our bodies produce a tremendous amount of internal heat. Under normal conditions, we cool ourselves by sweating and radiating heat through the skin. However, in certain circumstances, such as extreme heat, high humidity, or vigorous activity in the hot sun, this cooling system may begin to fail, allowing heat to build up to dangerous levels.

If a person becomes dehydrated and cannot sweat enough to cool their body, their internal temperature may rise to dangerously high levels, causing heat stroke. Symptoms include headache, mental confusion, and cramps throughout the entire body. If you have these symptoms, or notice them in a member of your hiking party, take immediate action to lower the body's core temperature. Get out of the sun and move to a shadier location. Pour water over the victim and fan the skin to stimulate sweating; sit in a nearby stream, if possible. Encourage the victim to drink liquids and rest. If symptoms are severe or don't improve within a few minutes of starting first aid, do not hesitate to call for help.

Probably the most effective way to cut risk for heat stroke is to stay adequately hydrated. When the temperatures soar on a New England summer day, stop frequently on the trail for water and rest breaks.

SPRAINS AND BREAKS
For any sprain or strain, remember RICE: rest, ice, compression, elevation. First, have the patient rest by lying down on the ground or nearest flat surface. Next, reduce swelling by gently placing a plastic freezer bag filled with cold water on the injury. To compress the ankle, snugly wrap the injury in an ACE bandage. (First-aid tape will also work.)

The wrap should cover the entire foot except for the heel and end several inches above the ankle. Most compression wraps are self-fastening or come with clip fasteners—or use tape to secure the end. If toes become purplish or blue, cool to the touch, or feel numb or tingly according to the patient, the wrap is too tight and should be loosened.

Keep the leg elevated until swelling is visibly reduced. When you or someone you are with suffers a sprained ankle or other minor injury on the trail, keep an open mind about finishing the hike. Because it's always more enjoyable when everyone can fully participate, it might be best to cut your losses and come back another time.

Navigational Tools

At some point, almost every hiker becomes lost. Torn down trail signs, trail detours, faded blazes, and snow, fog, and other conditions can make staying the course very rough going. First, take every step to prevent becoming lost. Before you hike, study a map of the area to become familiar with the trails, nearby roads, streams, mountains and other features. Leave a trip plan with family or friends and sign in at the trailhead register or nearby ranger cabin, if a hiker registry is available.

Always hike with a map and compass. And as you ramble along the trail, observe the topography around you (ridges, recognizable summits, rivers, etc.). They serve as good reference points, particularly when you are above the tree line. Some hikers leave small piles of rocks spaced at regular intervals to help them navigate treeless, alpine areas. Should you become disoriented, stop, pull out your map and look at the countryside for familiar landmarks.

Few people remain truly lost after consulting a map and calmly studying the terrain for five minutes. If you still need help orienting yourself, you may want to head to a ridge or high ground so you can identify hills or streams that are marked on your topographical map. Lay your map on the ground and put your compass on top to orient north. Another helpful gadget is an altimeter, which can tell you your approximate elevation; you can then pinpoint this elevation on a topographic map. Until you have your bearings, don't wander too far from your original route. If you told family members or fellow hikers where you plan to hike, that area is where rescuers will start searching for you.

Should you continue to be lost, S.T.O.P. (stop, think, observe, and plan). And don't panic. Not only does it cloud your judgment, you will be using up energy that you may need later on. Stay put and, if you carry a whistle, blow it at timed intervals to signal rescuers or other hikers (yelling also works).

HIKING ETHICS
Trail Etiquette

One of the great things about hiking is the quality of the people you meet on the trail. Hikers generally do not need an explanation of the value of courtesy, and one hopes this will always ring true. Still, with the popularity of hiking on the increase, and thousands of new hikers taking to the trails of New England every year, it's a good idea to brush up on some etiquette basics.

As a general rule and a friendly favor to other hikers, yield the trail to others whether you're going uphill or down. All trail users should yield to horses by stepping aside for the safety of everyone present. Likewise, horseback riders should, whenever possible, avoid situations where their animals are forced to push past hikers on very narrow trails.

Mountain bikers should yield to hikers, announce their approach, and pass nonbikers slowly. During hunting season, nonhunters should wear blaze orange, or an equally bright, conspicuous color. The hunters you may come across on the trail are usually responsible and friendly and deserve like treatment.

Many of us enjoy the woods and mountains for the quiet, and we should keep that in mind on the trail, at summits, or backcountry campsites. Many of us share the belief that things like cell phones, radios, and CD players do not belong in the mountains. High tech devices may also pose serious safety risks when used on the trail. Texting while hiking? Not a good idea when you should be watching out for exposed tree roots and rocky footing. Likewise, listening to a MP3 player could prevent you from hearing another hiker alerting you to dangers ahead.

New England has seen some conflict between hikers and mountain bikers, but it's important to remember that solutions to those issues are never reached through hostility and rudeness. Much more is accomplished when we begin from a foundation of mutual respect and courtesy. After all, we're all interested in preserving and enjoying our trails.

Large groups have a disproportionate impact on backcountry campsites and on the experience of other people. Be aware of and respect any restrictions on group size. Even where no regulation exists, keep your group size to no more than 10 people.

TIPS FOR AVOIDING CROWDS

Even on New England's most popular peaks, it is still possible to beat the crowds and have the trail all—or mostly—to yourself. Timing is everything. For hikes of less than six or seven miles round-trip, try to arrive at the trailhead early in the morning. Depending on the elevation gain, a seven-mile round-tripper will take the average hiker somewhere around three hours to complete—the perfect length for a late morning or early afternoon trek. Start your hike by 7 A.M. on a sunny Saturday morning and you will probably be returning to your car just as the weekend crush is arriving. For very short hikes, waiting until late afternoon or early evening before hitting the trail almost always ensures low boot traffic. But keep these late day hikes short and to destinations with easy footing just in case you're still out on the trail when night falls.

For very long hikes of nine miles round-trip or more, this early-bird strategy will not work, since early morning is the normal start time for most longer hikes. To still salvage a little solitude on your journey, you might want to consider breaking high mileage hikes into a two-day trek with an overnight stay at a shelter or backcountry campground. Start out on the trail later in the day and aim to camp at least halfway to the summit (within a mile of the summit is ideal). As early as you can the next day, finish the climb and enjoy the peaceful stillness.

Another way to avoid the crowds is to hike during the work week, when even the busiest of New England's trailheads are almost empty. If it felt as though you were part of a conga line climbing to the top of Mount Washington on a warm, sunny Sunday afternoon, come back on Wednesday and find almost no one around. Similarly, time your hikes according to the seasons. With the exception of a few places in northern New England that tend to stay muddy and even icy well into late spring, June is often the best month for encountering light boot traffic. Birds chirp, the air is fresh, wildflowers bloom in the meadows, and the throngs of summer tourists—and swarms of mosquitoes—have yet to arrive. Similarly, the week after Labor Day weekend is often quiet on the trail, with family vacationers gone back to school and the fall foliage season not yet underway.

Hiking with Children

Exploring the great outdoors with kids is one of life's great rewards. Starting from a very young age, a baby can be placed in a front carrier and taken out on almost any trail where the walking is flat and the environment serene; the rhythmic pace of hiking tends to lull even the fussiest of infants right to sleep. Backpack carriers are a good way to tote toddlers on-trail and, depending on the model, can accommodate a child of up to 35 pounds. When hiking with a child-carrier pack, keep a small mirror in your pocket so you can frequently check on your passenger without having to stop and remove the pack.

Around age three, kids are ready to hit the trail along with the rest of the family. But, little legs don't travel very far. Make your family outings kid-centric by picking short hikes that lead to such exciting features as waterfalls, duck-filled ponds, giant glacial erratics, huge gnarled tree trunks, beaver dams, and small hills with big views. Even if the hike is under a half mile in total length, plan extra time for rest stops and lots of unfettered exploration. Most children love the grown-up feel of having their own lightweight backpack; fill the pack with a water bottle and snack treats.

When a child reaches school age, physical ability rises dramatically. And so does his or her responsibility as a hiker. Teach your children how to read maps, how to use a compass, and what to do if lost. Show by example how to be courteous to the other hikers you encounter on the trail. Your efforts will be appreciated.

Hiking with Pets

Dogs are great trail companions and generally love the adventure of hiking every bit as much as their owners do. But dogs can create unnecessary friction in the backcountry. Dog owners should respect any regulations and not presume that strangers are eager to meet their pet. Keep your pet under physical control whenever other people are approaching. And for your dog's protection, always bring a leash along, even if regulations don't call for one.

Due to its large wildlife population, Baxter State Park in Maine is one notable destination that does not permit pets of any kind inside its borders. If you do have your dog along, check in with the campsites lining the access roads to Baxter. Many offer day boarding for dogs. Several bird refuges and Audubon sanctuaries also prohibit dogs. Call ahead to these and other destinations to find out trail regulations for pets.

Leave No Trace

Many of New England's trails receive heavy use, making it imperative that we all understand how to minimize our physical impact on the land. The nonprofit organization Leave No Trace (LNT) advocates a set of principles for low-impact backcountry use that are summarized in these basic guidelines:
- Be considerate of other visitors.
- Dispose of waste properly.
- Leave what you find.
- Minimize campfire impact.
- Plan ahead and prepare.

- Respect wildlife.
- Travel and camp on durable surfaces.

LNT offers more in-depth guidelines for low-impact camping and hiking on its website: www.lnt.org. You can also contact them by mail or phone: Leave No Trace Inc., P.O. Box 997, Boulder, CO 80306; 303/442-8222 or 800/332-4100.

Camping

The following are more recommendations that apply to many backcountry areas in New England:

- Avoid building campfires; cook with a backpacking stove. If you do build a campfire, use only wood found locally as a way to prevent the spread of destructive forest pests introduced from areas outside New England. In all six states, campers are encouraged not to move firewood more than 50 miles from its original source. Store-bought, packaged firewood is usually okay, as long as it is labeled "kiln dried" or "USDA Certified." Wood that is kiln dried is generally free of pests, although if the wood is not heated to a certain temperature, insects can survive.
- Avoid trails that are very muddy in spring; that's when they are most susceptible to erosion.
- Bury human waste beneath six inches of soil at least 200 feet from any water source.
- Burn and bury, or carry out, used toilet paper.
- Carry out everything you carry in.
- Choose a campsite at least 200 feet from trails and water sources, unless you're using a designated site. Make sure your site bears no evidence of your stay when you leave.
- Do not leave any food behind, even buried, as animals will dig it up. Learn how to hang food appropriately to keep it from bears. Black bears have spread their range over much of New England in recent years, and problems have arisen in isolated backcountry areas where human use is heavy.
- Even biodegradable soap is harmful to the environment, so simply wash your cooking gear with water away from any streams or ponds.
- Last but not least, know and follow any regulations for the area you will be visiting.

THE
NORTH WOODS

© JOHN "TJ AKA TEEJ" GORDON

BEST HIKES

◖ **Backpacking Hikes**
Russell Pond/Davis Pond Loop, **page 30.**
100-Mile Wilderness, **page 45.**
Half a 100-Mile Wilderness, **page 49.**

◖ **Kids**
Kidney Pond Loop, **page 43.**

◖ **Lakes and Swimming Holes**
Sandy Stream Pond/Whidden Ponds Loop,
   page 32.
Gulf Hagas, **page 51.**

◖ **Summit Hikes**
North Traveler Mountain, **page 27.**

If hiking in New England conjures images of

scaling mountains in the shadow of ski lifts or topping small hills with expansive views of rolling farmland, the trails found in Maine's North Woods stand out in sharp contrast. Here in this northernmost section of the state (east of U.S. 201 and north of Routes 2 and 9), the landscape is dominated by dense forest, wild lakes, roaming moose and bear, and mountain terrain that may seem more at home in rugged Alaska than genteel New England. Penetrating the very heart of this isolated region, the 26 hikes described in this chapter lie on public land and fall within two of Maine's greatest hiking areas: Baxter State Park and the 100-Mile Wilderness stretch of the Appalachian Trail.

With 204,733 acres remaining as close to true wilderness as managed lands come, Baxter is Maine's flagship state park. It provides a hiking experience that's rare in New England: remote and untamed. Maine's highest peak, 5,267-foot Mount Katahdin, dominates the park's south end and attracts the bulk of hiker traffic. It's legendary as the northern terminus of the Appalachian Trail and the home of the Knife Edge, the fin-like glacial ridge often dubbed, "the longest mile in Maine." Baxter State Park boasts more than 47 other peaks, including standouts Mount Coe, Doubletop, the Owl, the Brothers, and the Traveler, a massive ancient volcano along the park's northeastern boundary. Away from the summits, Baxter's many trails take visitors to waterfalls, ponds, and deep into the woods where the potential is high for a close encounter with moose, bears, beavers, foxes, and countless other forms of northern wildlife.

At busy times in the summer, some parking lots at popular trailheads — usually Katahdin trails — fill up, and the park will not allow any more vehicles in those lots on that day, effectively forcing visitors who come later to choose other trailheads and hikes. There are no overflow parking areas, but trailhead parking north of Katahdin rarely fills, so you can always find someplace to hike. The park's Tote Road is not open to vehicles in winter and access by ski or snowshoe is required. Millinocket Road is maintained in winter as far as Abol Bridge Campground; the road to the park's Matagamon Gate entrance is maintained only as far as a private campground about four miles east of the gate.

The 100-Mile Wilderness stretch of the Appalachian Trail is neither officially designated federal wilderness nor true wilderness as found in the American West or Alaska — you may hear the distant thrum of logging machinery while hiking here. But the Wilderness does offer some of the most remote hiking in all New England, and the big lakes here are home to loons and many other birds and are a favorite haunt of moose. The 100-Mile Wilderness stretch is also the longest hike you can do on trail in the region without crossing a paved or public road (it does, however, cross several logging roads). The busiest months in the Wilderness are August and September, when you're likely to encounter lots of other backpackers, though still not as many as on popular White Mountains trails.

The hiking season begins with the disappearance of snow in late spring — though the black flies, no-see-ums, and mosquitoes also emerge — and extends into October, when the first snow may start flying. There are no public water sources in Baxter State Park or along the 100-Mile Wilderness; treat your water or bring an adequate supply with you. Advance reservations for Baxter State Park campground sites and backcountry campsites are essential and should be made many months in advance of your trip. Along the 100-Mile Wilderness, lean-tos are on a first come, first served basis; low impact camping is allowed along this stretch of the AT.

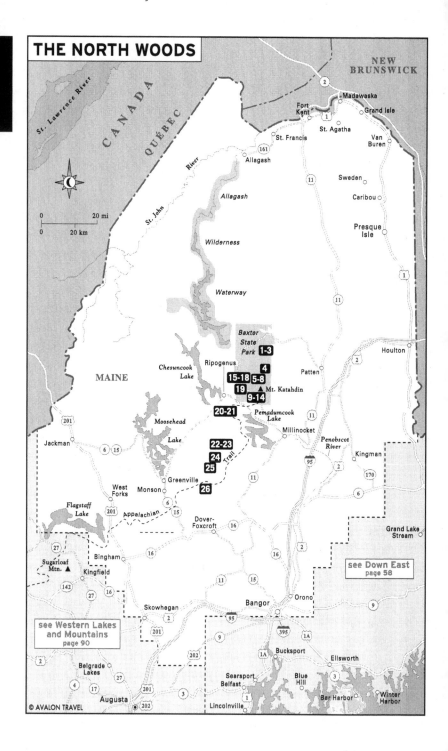

1 SOUTH BRANCH FALLS
1 mi/1 hr

in northern Baxter State Park

A scenic leg stretcher after the long drive to Baxter, the South Branch Falls Trail, near South Branch Pond Campground, is a short, easy trek to cascading waterfalls along South Branch Pond Brook.

Pick up the trailhead at a small turnoff parking area on the west side of South Branch Pond Road, approximately 1.3 miles south of the Tote Road junction. Follow the blue blazes and descend gently through a mixed forest of dense poplar and birch (a good place to test the effectiveness of the bug repellant you've hopefully applied). As the sound of rushing water grows louder, the trail (at 0.4 mile) makes a sudden—and steep—descent out of the woods and into the deep ravine carved out by the South Falls Pond Brook. Carefully make your way along a series of rocky ledges as the trail takes you down to the brook and the falls. The falls appear as a series of cascades formed by water shooting out from between the ledges. The largest fall drops four feet and forms an inviting pool—the perfect spot for a quick dip. Other short side trails take you to different viewing points along the picturesque ravine. Return the way you came.

User Groups: Hikers only. No dogs, horses, mountain bikes, or wheelchair facilities.

Permits: No permits required. An entrance fee of $13 per vehicle is charged at the gatehouse, but vehicles bearing Maine registration enter at no charge. Parking in the park is free.

Maps: A waterproof trail map of Baxter State Park is available from the Appalachian Mountain Club (Rangeley–Stratton/Baxter State Park–Katahdin map, $7.95). For a topographic map, request Wassataquoik Lake and the Traveler from the USGS.

Directions: Trailhead is most easily accessed using Baxter State Park's northern Matagamon Gate entrance. From the junction of Routes 11 and 159 in Patten, drive west on Route 159 (Shin Pond Road) for 10 miles. At Shin Pond, Route 159 becomes Grand Lake Road, a private park access road that is open for public use. Stay on Grand Lake Road, following the road for 14 miles to reach the entrance for Baxter State Park. From the gatehouse, drive 7.3 miles along Tote Road (the park's perimeter road) and turn left at the sign for South Branch Pond Campground. Drive 1.3 miles to a parking turnout on the right.

Baxter State Park is open May 15–November 1 and December 1–March 31. During the summer season, the Matagamon Gate is open 6 A.M.–10 P.M.; the park's Togue Pond Gate is open 6 A.M.–10 P.M.—though it may open as early as 5 A.M. at the discretion of the park director.

GPS Coordinates: 46.1155 N, 68.9070 W

Contact: Baxter State Park, 64 Balsam Dr., Millinocket, ME 04462-2190, 207/723-5140, www.baxterstateparkauthority.com.

2 NORTH TRAVELER MOUNTAIN
5 mi/3.5 hr

in northern Baxter State Park

BEST (

The superstar of Baxter's northern mountains is the Traveler (3,541 ft.), a sprawling, five-peaked ancient volcano rising high above Pogy Notch. North Traveler (3,144 ft.) is the most popular of the Traveler summits and its trailhead is easily accessed from the South Branch Pond Campground. With much of the mountain left denuded by a massive fire over a century ago, North Traveler is a rugged, somewhat rocky climb along mostly uncovered ridges. A total elevation gain of more than 2,000 feet, North Traveler's sweeping views rank among Baxter's most scenic.

From the South Branch Pond Campground parking area, walk the road into the campground. North Traveler defines the skyline to the east, or left, just above the Lower South Branch Pond. Bear left after entering the campground and pass several sites before reaching a large signpost for the Pogy Notch trailhead. Here, turn right (south) and follow Pogy Notch 0.1 mile to a well-marked trail junction. North Traveler Trail is to the left, a blue-blazed trail that begins with a fairly steep ascent along the edge of North Ridge (Pogy Notch is also blue-blazed, so be sure to look for the North Traveler Trail sign). Less than a half mile from the trailhead, forest cover ends and the trail emerges onto open ledges with excellent views of the two South Branch Ponds, across to the South Branch Mountains, and south toward Katahdin. The vistas only improve as you continue up the uncovered ridge, but loose stones and areas of rocky terrain can make footing difficult (especially around the 0.8 mile mark). After leveling out for a short stretch, the trail climbs again, passing through a grove of stunted birch trees and eventually to a luscious upland meadow (at 2.0 miles). Continue following the blazes and cairns to the broad summit, where stunning views are seen in every direction, including north to the wilderness and south to the main summit of the Traveler. Descend the way you came.

User Groups: Hikers only. No dogs, horses, mountain bikes, or wheelchair facilities. Trail should not be attempted in winter except by hikers experienced in mountaineering and prepared for severe weather; not suitable for skis.

Permits: No permits required. An entrance fee of $13 per vehicle is charged at the gatehouse, but vehicles bearing Maine registration enter at no charge. Parking in the park is free.

Maps: A waterproof trail map of Baxter State Park is available from the Appalachian Mountain Club (Rangeley–Stratton/Baxter State Park–Katahdin map, $7.95). For a topographic map, request Wassataquoik Lake and the Traveler from the USGS.

Directions: The trailhead is most easily accessed using Baxter State Park's northern Matagamon Gate entrance. From the junction of Routes 11 and 159 in Patten, drive west on Route 159 (Shin Pond Road) for 10 miles. At Shin Pond, Route 159 becomes Grand Lake Road, a private access road that is open for public use. Stay on Grand Lake Road, following the road for 14 miles to reach the entrance of Baxter State Park. From the gatehouse, drive 7.3 miles along Tote Road (the park's perimeter road) and turn left at the sign for South Branch Pond Campground. Drive 2.3 miles to the parking area at the end of the road.

Baxter State Park is open May 15–November 1 and December 1–March 31. During the summer season, the Matagamon Gate is open 6 a.m.–10 p.m.; the park's Togue Pond Gate is open 6 a.m.–10 p.m.—though it may open as early as 5 a.m. at the discretion of the park director. The road is not maintained to the trailhead in winter.

GPS Coordinates: 46.1079 N, 68.8979 W

Contact: Baxter State Park, 64 Balsam Dr., Millinocket, ME 04462-2190, 207/723-5140, www.baxterstateparkauthority.com.

❸ TRAVELER LOOP
10.5 mi/10 hr   🏃5 ⛰10

in northern Baxter State Park

The Traveler (3,541 ft.), along Baxter's northeast boundary, is a rocky, exposed mountain rivaled only by Katahdin for its unique features, stunning views, and difficulty in climbing—the loose rock found so abundantly here quickly becomes treacherous when wet. Bagging three of the mountain's five peaks, including the Traveler's tallest summit, this loop hike makes use of one of the park's newest trails, the challenging Traveler Trail. Opened in 2005, Traveler Trail connects Peak of the Ridges (3,225 ft.) with the Traveler's main summit and then turns north to reach the North Traveler summit (3,152 ft.). Because of the hike's length, you will want to start this one very early in the day. The complete loop nets an elevation gain of 3,700 feet from the Pogy Notch trailhead.

Leaving the South Branch Pond

Campground parking area, walk the road into the campground. Bear left after entering camp and pass several campsites before reaching a large signpost for the Pogy Notch Trail. Turn right (south) onto the blue-blazed Pogy Notch Trail. After a mile, the trail passes a junction with the Howe Brook Trail and then crosses an often-dry streambed. Reach another trail junction at 1.5 miles and turn left onto the Center Ridge Trail (also blue-blazed). Begin with a relentless and steep climb over loose rock for the first 0.7 mile. The ascent then levels out as the trail makes a more gradual climb up an open ridge. Enjoy magnificent views of the two South Branch Ponds, across to the South Branch Mountains and south toward Katahdin. At 1.2 miles, the trail becomes rocky and somewhat steep again, forcing you to scramble across an extensive talus field to reach the Peak of the Ridges summit, 2.1 miles from the Center Ridge trailhead.

Leave the summit via the Traveler Trail (blue-blazed), descending east along a sharp ridge of exposed volcanic rhyolite. At 0.7 mile from the Traveler trailhead, reach a large alpine meadow. At the meadow's eastern edge, the trail begins the ascent towards the Traveler summit, pushing its way up a steep talus slope before reaching the mountain's highest peak, a total hiking distance of 1.4 miles from Peak of the Ridges. On the open summit, enjoy panoramic views in all directions, including south to Katahdin and north into the wilderness. To reach North Traveler, the Traveler Trail continues north for another 2.9 miles. Leaving the summit, the trail descends, losing a total elevation of 800 feet over the next half mile. A forested col awaits at the end of this downward progression and the beginning of another long, rocky ridge—the trail's ascent to North Traveler starts here. Completely above the tree line all the way to the North Traveler peak, the views are expansive in all directions. The Traveler Trail ends at North Traveler summit. Return to the campground using the North Traveler and Pogy Notch trails (see *North Traveler Mountain* listing in this chapter).

User Groups: Hikers only. No dogs, horses, mountain bikes, or wheelchair facilities. Trail should not be attempted in winter except by hikers experienced in mountaineering and prepared for severe weather; not suitable for skis.

Permits: No permits required. An entrance fee of $13 per vehicle is charged at the gatehouse, but vehicles bearing Maine registration enter at no charge. Parking in the park is free.

Maps: A waterproof trail map of Baxter State Park is available from the Appalachian Mountain Club (Rangeley–Stratton/Baxter State Park–Katahdin map, $7.95). For a topographic map, request Wassataquoik Lake and the Traveler from the USGS.

Directions: Trailhead is most easily accessed using Baxter State Park's northern Matagamon Gate entrance. From the junction of Routes 11 and 159 in Patten, drive west on Route 159 (Shin Pond Road) for 10 miles. At Shin Pond, Route 159 becomes Grand Lake Road, a private access road that is open for public use. Stay on Grand Lake Road, following the road for 14 miles to reach the entrance of Baxter State Park. From the gatehouse, drive for 7.3 miles along Tote Road (the park's perimeter road) and turn left at the sign for South Branch Pond Campground. Drive 2.3 miles to the parking area at the end of the road.

Baxter State Park is open May 15–November 1 and December 1–March 31. During the summer season, the Matagamon Gate is open 6 A.M.–10 P.M.; the park's Togue Pond Gate is open 6 A.M.–10 P.M.—though it may open as early as 5 A.M. at the discretion of the park director. The road is not maintained to the trailhead in winter.

GPS Coordinates: 46.1079 N, 68.8979 W

Contact: Baxter State Park, 64 Balsam Dr., Millinocket, ME 04462-2190, 207/723-5140, www.baxterstateparkauthority.com.

4 RUSSELL POND/DAVIS POND LOOP

19 mi/3 days   🥾4 ⛰9

In central Baxter State Park

BEST (

Visitors to this magnificent park who hike only Katahdin—especially on a busy summer weekend—may not get a true sense of Baxter's remoteness. This loop, spread out over three days to take advantage of two excellent backcountry camping areas at Russell and Davis Ponds, wanders away from the park's popular peaks and brings you deep into the wilderness and solitude of Baxter's central section. The only steep stretches of this hike are the climbs to Davis Pond in the Northwest Basin and above Davis Pond to the Northwest Plateau, and the descent off Hamlin Peak. Much of this loop is easy hiking that fit backpackers can accomplish in a few hours of hiking per day.

From the parking area at Roaring Brook Campground, walk past the ranger's cabin and follow a well-worn path for about fifty yards to the trail junction. Russell Pond Trail turns right and is a relatively flat seven-mile hike north to Russell Pond Campground. A ranger is on duty at Russell Pond and canoe rentals are available. Listen for early morning or evening splashes in the pond—it's probably a moose grazing on some underwater foliage.

Day two, the hike follows the Northwest Basin Trail. To find the trailhead, double back on the Russell Pond Trail for 0.1 mile to reach a trail junction—take Northwest Basin Trail on the right (heading southwest). Climb gradually for the next five miles, passing such trail features as rock-strewn Wassataquoik Stream, the site of an old logging camp, and a large heath-covered knoll, a glacial *roche moutonnée*. At 5.2 miles, and about 1,700 feet uphill, is the Davis Pond lean-to (sleeps four).

The final day takes you up the Northwest Basin Trail onto the rocky, alpine Northwest Plateau area. At 2.2 miles past Davis Pond, come to a trail junction. Turn left onto the

Hamlin Ridge Trail, soon passing over Hamlin Peak (4,751 ft.), one of Maine's 14 4,000-footers. The trail then descends along the open, rocky Hamlin Ridge, heading almost due east. Enjoy constant views down into the soaring, cliff-ringed North Basin to your left (north) and toward Katahdin on the right (south). About two miles from Hamlin Peak, reach a trail junction with the North Basin Trail. Turn left, following the North Basin Trail a short distance to the junction with the North Basin Cutoff. Here, turn right and follow the cutoff a bit more than a half mile to the Chimney Pond Trail. Turn left and follow the Chimney Pond Trail another 2.3 miles back to Roaring Brook Campground.

Advance reservations for campsites are strongly recommended. Russell Pond has a bunkhouse (capacity 13), four tent sites, and four lean-tos (capacity 4–8); Davis Pond has one lean-to (capacity 4).

User Groups: Hikers only. No dogs, horses, mountain bikes, or wheelchair facilities. This trail should not be attempted in winter.

Permits: No permits required. An entrance fee of $13 per vehicle is charged at the gatehouse, but vehicles bearing Maine registration can enter at no charge. Parking in the park is free.

Maps: A waterproof trail map of Baxter State Park is available from the Appalachian Mountain Club (Rangeley–Stratton/Baxter State Park–Katahdin map, $7.95). For a topographic map, ask the USGS for Mount Katahdin and Katahdin Lake.

Directions: From Millinocket, head west on Central Street/Route 11/Route 157 toward State Street. Turn right at Katahdin Avenue and follow briefly before turning left at Bates Street. This street becomes Millinocket Road. After 7.4 miles, bear right at a fork onto Baxter Park Road. Follow another 8.4 miles before reaching the park's Togue Pond gate. Just beyond the gatehouse, take the right fork on the gravel Tote Road (the park's perimeter road) and drive 8.1 miles to Roaring Brook Campground. The Russell Pond Trail begins beside the ranger station (where there is a hiker register).

Baxter State Park is open May 15–November 1 and December 1–March 31. During the summer season, the park's Togue Pond Gate is open 6 A.M.–10 P.M.—though it may open at 5 A.M. at the discretion of the park director; the Matagamon Gate is open 6 A.M.–10 P.M. GPS Coordinates: 45.9204 N, 68.8577 W **Contact:** Baxter State Park, 64 Balsam Dr., Millinocket, ME 04462-2190, 207/723-5140, www.baxterstateparkauthority.com.

5 SOUTH TURNER MOUNTAIN
4 mi/3 hr   🏃4 ⛰9

in southern Baxter State Park

Though just 3,122 feet in elevation, South Turner's craggy summit gives a rare view of the entire Katahdin massif from the east side. Be prepared to spot moose and other wildlife, but not too many people, en route to the top of this mountain near Sandy Stream Pond. South Turner is so overshadowed by the big mountain to the southwest that many hikers don't even know about it—enhancing your chances of summiting in solitude. A scenically rewarding hike, the South Turner Trail is a moderate climb of 1,638 feet from the trailhead at Roaring Brook Campground.

Leaving the parking area near the ranger station at Roaring Brook Campground, follow the Russell Pond Trail north for a quarter mile to reach a trail junction. Turn right to follow the South Turner Mountain/Sandy Stream Pond Trail. You soon reach Sandy Stream Pond's southeast shore, which the trail follows (be on the lookout for moose and other wildlife in the early morning or evening hours). Coming around to the pond's far end (0.7 mile from Roaring Brook Campground), the South Turner Mountain Trail turns right and soon begins a steep climb through dense forest. Approaching the summit, the trail's final

stretch breaks out of the trees to unparalleled views of Katahdin's open cirques. Descend the same way you came.

User Groups: Hikers only. No dogs, horses, mountain bikes, or wheelchair facilities. This trail may be difficult to snowshoe in winter and is not suitable for skis.

Permits: No permits required. An entrance fee of $13 per vehicle is charged at the gatehouse, but vehicles bearing Maine registration can enter at no charge.

Maps: A waterproof trail map of Baxter State Park is available from the Appalachian Mountain Club (Rangeley–Stratton/Baxter State Park–Katahdin map, $7.95). For a topographic map, ask the USGS for Mount Katahdin and Katahdin Lake.

Directions: From Millinocket, head west on Central Street/Route 11/Route 157 toward State Street. Turn right at Katahdin Avenue and follow briefly before turning left at Bates Street. This street becomes Millinocket Road. After 7.4 miles, bear right at the fork for Baxter Park Road. Follow another 8.4 miles before reaching the park's Togue Pond gate. Just beyond the gatehouse, take the right fork on the gravel Tote Road (the park's perimeter road) and drive 8.1 miles to Roaring Brook Campground. The Russell Pond Trail begins beside the ranger station (where there is a hiker register).

Baxter State Park is open May 15–November 1 and December 1–March 31. During the summer season, the park's Togue Pond Gate is open 6 A.M.–10 P.M.—though it may open at 5 A.M. at the discretion of the park director; the Matagamon Gate is open 6 A.M.–10 P.M. The road is not maintained to the trailhead in winter, but it can be skied. GPS Coordinates: 45.9204 N, 68.8577 W **Contact:** Baxter State Park, 64 Balsam Dr., Millinocket, ME 04462-2190, 207/723-5140, www.baxterstateparkauthority.com.

6 SANDY STREAM POND/ WHIDDEN PONDS LOOP

2.3 mi/1 hr

in southern Baxter State Park

BEST (

This relatively flat, easy loop near Roaring Brook Campground hits two ponds where moose are often seen, especially early in the morning or around dusk (when the animals are most active). Mainly a hike to take in the natural beauty of Baxter's unspoiled pond ecosystems, the ramble leads to a terrific view across the southernmost of the Whidden Ponds toward the North Basin of Hamlin and Howe Peaks. Beginning in early September, the hardwood forest of birch, ash, and beech ringing the ponds blazes with autumn color, a nice contrast to Baxter's almost unbroken sea of evergreens. Hike this loop in the morning or afternoon if you seek solitude, as pond trails are popular early evening strolls for campers at Roaring Brook.

From the ranger station at Roaring Brook Campground, follow the Russell Pond Trail a brief 0.1 mile, turning right at a marked junction onto the South Turner Mountain Trail/ Sandy Stream Pond Trail. The trail hugs the southeast shore of Sandy Stream Pond, with short spur trails leading to picturesque viewing points. As you come around the far end of the pond, the South Turner Mountain Trail leads right; this hike turns left onto the Whidden Pond Trail, following it for a mile to the first of the Whidden Ponds (also the largest and the only one directly accessed by a trail). The trail ends at a junction with the Russell Pond Trail, but you can still see more of Whidden Pond. Turn right and follow the Russell Pond Trail for 0.2 mile, walking along the shore for views toward North Basin. Turn back (south) on the Russell Pond Trail for an easy one-mile hike back to Roaring Brook Campground.

User Groups: Hikers only. No dogs, horses, mountain bikes, or wheelchair facilities. This trail should not be attempted in winter except by experienced skiers or snowshoers prepared for severe winter weather.

Permits: No permits required. An entrance fee of $13 per vehicle is charged at the gatehouse, but vehicles bearing Maine registration can enter at no charge.

Maps: A waterproof trail map of Baxter State Park is available from the Appalachian Mountain Club (Rangeley–Stratton/Baxter State Park–Katahdin map, $7.95). For a topographic map, ask the USGS for Mount Katahdin and Katahdin Lake.

Directions: From Millinocket, head west on Central Street/Route 11/Route 157 toward State Street. Turn right at Katahdin Avenue and follow briefly before turning left at Bates Street. This street becomes Millinocket Road. After 7.4 miles, bear right at the fork for Baxter Park Road. Follow another 8.4 miles before reaching the park's Togue Pond gate. Just beyond the gatehouse, take the right fork on the gravel Tote Road (the park's perimeter road) and drive 8.1 miles to Roaring Brook Campground. The Russell Pond Trail begins beside the ranger station (where there is a hiker register).

Baxter State Park is open May 15–November 1 and December 1–March 31. During the summer season, the park's Togue Pond Gate is open 6 A.M.–10 P.M.—though it may open at 5 A.M. at the discretion of the park director; the Matagamon Gate is open 6 A.M.–10 P.M. The road is not maintained to the trailhead in winter, but it can be skied.

GPS Coordinates: 45.9204 N, 68.8577 W

Contact: Baxter State Park, 64 Balsam Dr., Millinocket, ME 04462-2190, 207/723-5140, www.baxterstateparkauthority.com.

7 HAMLIN PEAK

10.2 mi/6 hr

in southern Baxter State Park

Hamlin Peak, at 4,751 feet, is Maine's second highest peak and one of 14 4,000-footers in the state, though it's also considered part of the Katahdin massif. Swarms of hikers climb Katahdin on summer weekends, but far fewer venture up onto Hamlin—and they are missing a lot. The constant views along the Hamlin Ridge, both into the North Basin and back toward the South Basin and Katahdin, are among the most magnificent in Baxter. This 9.5-mile round-trip hike climbs about 3,200 feet in elevation and is fairly strenuous.

From Roaring Brook Campground, follow the Chimney Pond Trail an easy 2.3 miles to a trail junction just beyond the Basin Ponds. Turn right onto the North Basin Cutoff, which ascends steadily for approximately 0.6 mile before coming to another junction. A short distance to the right (0.1 mile) is Blueberry Knoll and views into the North Basin. Experienced hikers will see that it's possible to bushwhack down to the pair of tiny ponds on the North Basin floor and explore that rugged glacial cirque. This hike, however, turns left (southwest) onto the North Basin Trail. Follow the North Basin Trail for 0.2 mile and then take a right to begin ascending the Hamlin Ridge Trail. Two miles farther you reach Hamlin Peak, a mound of rocks slightly higher than the vast surrounding tableland, or plateau. Descend the way you came.

Special note: For visitors making this peak part of an extended stay at Baxter State Park, another enjoyable way of hiking Hamlin is from Chimney Pond Campground, which is 3.3 miles from Roaring Brook Campground via the Chimney Pond Trail. Backpack in to Chimney Pond, and hike Hamlin Peak via the Chimney Pond, North Basin, and Hamlin Ridge trails (four miles, 2.5 hours). Chimney Pond is a good staging point for hikes of Katahdin, or even for beginning the Russell Pond/Davis Pond backpacking loop in the reverse direction.

User Groups: Hikers only. No dogs, horses, mountain bikes, or wheelchair facilities. This trail should not be attempted in winter except by experienced skiers or snowshoers prepared for severe winter weather.

Permits: No permits required. An entrance fee of $13 per vehicle is charged at the gatehouse, but vehicles bearing Maine registration can enter at no charge.

Maps: A waterproof trail map of Baxter State Park is available from the Appalachian Mountain Club (Rangeley–Stratton/Baxter State Park–Katahdin map, $7.95). For a topographic map, ask the USGS for Mount Katahdin and Katahdin Lake.

Directions: From Millinocket, head west on Central Street/Route 11/Route 157 toward State Street. Turn right at Katahdin Avenue and follow briefly before turning left at Bates Street. This street becomes Millinocket Road. After 7.4 miles, bear right at the fork for Baxter Park Road. Follow another 8.4 miles before reaching the park's Togue Pond gate. Just beyond the gatehouse, take the right fork on the gravel Tote Road (the park's perimeter road) and drive 8.1 miles to Roaring Brook Campground. The Chimney Pond Trail begins beside the ranger station (where there is a hiker register).

Baxter State Park is open May 15–November 1 and December 1–March 31. During the summer season, the park's Togue Pond Gate is open 6 A.M.–10 P.M.—though it may open at 5 A.M. at the discretion of the park director; the Matagamon Gate is open 6 A.M.–10 P.M. The road is not maintained to the trailhead in winter, but it can be skied.

GPS Coordinates: 45.9204 N, 68.8577 W

Contact: Baxter State Park, 64 Balsam Dr., Millinocket, ME 04462-2190, 207/723-5140, www.baxterstateparkauthority.com.

8 KATAHDIN: KNIFE EDGE LOOP

9.3 mi/9 hr

In southern Baxter State Park

Truly a mountain experience like no other in New England, this hike is the best way to take in as much of Maine's greatest mountain as possible in a day. Offering an elevation gain of 3,800 feet and made up almost entirely of rugged terrain, the loop encompasses Chimney Pond (set deep in the vast glacial cirque known as the South Basin), a challenging scramble up the Cathedral Trail, Katahdin's four peaks, the infamous Knife Edge arête, and the open Keep Ridge. Don't underestimate its length, difficulty, or dangers: Since the park started keeping records in 1926, 44 hiker deaths have occurred on Katahdin, usually the result of falls or lightning strikes.

High atop Katahdin's South Basin, hikers negotiate the narrow, rocky terrain of the Knife Edge Trail.

From the parking area at Roaring Brook Campground, follow the fairly easy Chimney Pond Trail 3.3 miles east to the pond camping area (many visitors make this hike and go no farther because the views from Chimney Pond are so beautiful). Behind the Chimney Pond ranger station, pick up the Cathedral Trail, which climbs steeply up a rockslide and the right flank of Katahdin's sweeping head wall, passing the three prominent stone buttresses known as the Cathedrals. You can scramble off trail onto each of the Cathedrals for great South Basin views.

At 1.4 miles from the Cathedral trailhead, bear left where the trail forks, soon reaching a junction (in 0.1 miles) with the Saddle Trail and the more level ground of the Katahdin Tableland (at 1.5 miles). Turn left (southeast) onto the Saddle Trail and walk 0.2 mile to the main summit, Baxter Peak, where a large sign marks the highest point in Maine (5,267 ft.) and the Appalachian Trail's northern terminus. If high winds or the threat of thunderstorms have not forced rangers to temporarily close the next leg of the loop, continue straight over the summit (southeast) and onto the Knife Edge Trail, an increasingly narrow, rocky ridge that runs 1.1 miles across the top of South Basin to Pamola Peak. The Knife Edge Trail first hooks left to reach South Peak before beginning the precipitous 0.8-mile stretch to Pamola Peak. At times, the footpath is barely two feet wide, with sharp drops to either side. At Chimney Peak, scramble down the vertical wall of a ridge cleft, a spot known

to intimidate more than a few hikers. Then you scramble up the other side (not as difficult) onto Pamola Peak. From here, turn right (east) on the Helon Taylor Trail, which descends the Keep Ridge, much of it open, for 3.1 miles to the Chimney Pond Trail. Turn right and walk 0.1 mile back to Roaring Brook Campground.

User Groups: Hikers only. No dogs, horses, mountain bikes, or wheelchair facilities. This trail should not be attempted in winter except by hikers experienced in mountaineering and prepared for severe winter weather, and is only suitable for skis as far as Chimney Pond.

Permits: No permits required. An entrance fee of $13 per vehicle is charged at the gatehouse, but vehicles bearing Maine registration can enter at no charge.

Maps: A waterproof trail map of Baxter State Park is available from the Appalachian Mountain Club (Rangeley–Stratton/Baxter State Park–Katahdin map, $7.95). For a topographic map, ask the USGS for Mount Katahdin and Katahdin Lake.

Directions: From Millinocket, head west on Central Street/Route 11/Route 157 toward State Street. Turn right at Katahdin Avenue and follow briefly before turning left at Bates Street. This street becomes Millinocket Road. After 7.4 miles, bear right at the fork for Baxter Park Road. Follow another 8.4 miles before reaching the park's Togue Pond gate. Just beyond the gatehouse, take the right fork on the gravel Tote Road (the park's perimeter road) and drive 8.1 miles to Roaring Brook Campground. The Chimney Pond Trail begins beside the ranger station (where there is a hiker register).

Baxter State Park is open May 15–November 1 and December 1–March 31. During the summer season, the park's Togue Pond Gate is open 6 A.M.–10 P.M.—though it may open at 5 A.M. at the discretion of the park director; the Matagamon Gate is open 6 A.M.–10 P.M. The road is not maintained to the trailhead in winter, but it can be skied.

GPS Coordinates: 45.9204 N, 68.8577 W

Contact: Baxter State Park, 64 Balsam Dr., Millinocket, ME 04462-2190, 207/723-5140, www.baxterstateparkauthority.com.

9 KATAHDIN: SADDLE TRAIL
11 mi/7 hr 🏃5 ⛺10

in southern Baxter State Park

By using the high plateau of the Katahdin Tableland for almost half its ascent to Baxter Peak (5,267 ft.), the Saddle Trail, a total climb of 2,353 feet from its trailhead at Chimney Pond Campground, is the most gradual approach to the top of Katahdin. The strenuous part of this summit trail comes at the very beginning—a steep scramble up the loose gravel and rock of the Saddle Slide.

From the Roaring Brook Campground parking area, proceed into the campground to pick up the westbound Chimney Pond Trail (look for the large trail signpost in the middle of the camp near the ranger's station). Follow the well-worn trail, a former tote road, for 3.3 miles to Chimney Pond Campground (2,914 ft.). Find the Saddle trailhead near the ranger's station in the middle of the campground (look for the large trail signpost) and proceed west. The blue-blazed trail ascends gradually through dense conifer cover before breaking out of the woods (at 1.0 mile) and

beginning the steep ascent up the Saddle Slide. It's a vigorous scramble for the next 0.2 mile as you make your way among giant granite boulders and loose rock, the result of a landslide that took place in 1893. Pay attention to your footing and keep an eye on the progress of those ahead of you—accidentally dislodge a rock and it's easy to send a sizeable stone hurtling down towards an unsuspecting hiker. Reaching the Tableland (4,300 ft.), the trail soon comes to a junction. Bear left to stay on the Saddle Trail and continue one more mile towards Baxter Peak, passing two other trail junctions before standing on Katahdin's summit. Return the way you came.

User Groups: Hikers only. No wheelchair facilities. Bikes, dogs, and horses are prohibited. This trail should not be attempted in winter except by hikers experienced in mountaineering and prepared for severe winter weather, and is only suitable for skis as far as Chimney Pond.

Permits: No permits required. An entrance fee of $13 per vehicle is charged at the gatehouse, but vehicles bearing Maine registration can enter at no charge.

Maps: A waterproof trail map of Baxter State Park is available from the Appalachian Mountain Club (Rangeley–Stratton/Baxter State Park–Katahdin map, $7.95). For a topographic map, ask the USGS for Mount Katahdin and Katahdin Lake.

Directions: From Millinocket, head west on Central Street/Route 11/Route 157 toward State Street. Turn right at Katahdin Avenue and follow briefly before turning left at Bates Street. This street becomes Millinocket Road. After 7.4 miles, bear right at the fork for Baxter Park Road. Follow another 8.4 miles before reaching the park's Togue Pond gate. Just beyond the gatehouse, take the right fork on the gravel Tote Road (the park's perimeter road) and drive 8.1 miles to the parking area at Roaring Brook Campground. The Chimney Pond Trail begins beside the ranger station (where there is a hiker register).

Baxter State Park is open May 15–November

1 and December 1–March 31. During the summer season, the park's Togue Pond Gate opens is open 6 A.M.–10 P.M.—though it may open at 5 A.M. at the discretion of the park director; the Matagamon Gate is open 6 A.M.–10 P.M. The road is not maintained to the trailhead in winter, but it can be skied. GPS Coordinates: 45.9159 N, 68.9126 W

Contact: Baxter State Park, 64 Balsam Dr., Millinocket, ME 04462-2190, 207/723-5140, www.baxterstateparkauthority.com.

10 KATAHDIN: ABOL TRAIL
7.6 mi/7 hr   🥾5 ⛰10

in southern Baxter State Park

This trail follows the path of the 1816 Abol landslide, and may be the oldest existing route up the 5,267-foot Katahdin. Ascending the massif from the southwest, Abol Trail is the shortest way to Katahdin's main summit, Baxter Peak, but by no means easy: It climbs 4,000 feet, and the slide's steepness and loose rock make for an arduous ascent, complicated by the possibility of falling rock. And descending this trail is harder than going up, though not impossible (but it can be very rough going on the knees).

From the Abol Campground day-use parking area, find the prominently marked Abol trailhead at the northern end of the campground. The trail leads through woods for more than a mile to the broad slide base. Pick your way carefully up the slide; watch for falling rock caused by hikers above, and take care not to kick anything down onto hikers below. At 2.6 miles, the trail reaches the level ground of the Tableland, a beautiful, sprawling alpine plateau. At 2.8 miles, near Thoreau Spring, the blue-blazed Abol Trail connects with the Hunt Trail. Turn right on the white-blazed Hunt Trail for the final mile to Baxter Peak, both Katahdin's summit and the Appalachian Trail's northern terminus. By shuttling vehicles between Abol and Katahdin Stream Campgrounds, you can ascend the Abol and descend the Hunt Trail (adding 1.4 miles to your trek). Otherwise, descend the way you came.

User Groups: Hikers only. No wheelchair facilities. Bikes, dogs, and horses are prohibited. This trail should not be attempted in winter except by hikers experienced in mountaineering and prepared for severe winter weather; not suitable for skis.

Permits: No permits required. An entrance fee of $13 per vehicle is charged at the gatehouse, but vehicles bearing Maine registration can enter at no charge.

Maps: A waterproof trail map of Baxter State Park is available from the Appalachian Mountain Club (Rangeley–Stratton/Baxter State Park–Katahdin map, $7.95). For a topographic map, ask the USGS for Mount Katahdin and Katahdin Lake.

Directions: From Millinocket, head west on Central Street/Route 11/Route 157 toward State Street. Turn right at Katahdin Avenue and follow briefly before turning left at Bates Street. This street becomes Millinocket Road. After 7.4 miles, bear right at the fork for Baxter Park Road. Follow another 8.4 miles before reaching the park's Togue Pond gate. Just beyond the gatehouse, take the right fork on the gravel Tote Road (the park's perimeter road) and drive 5.7 miles to Abol Campground and day-use parking on the left, opposite the campground entrance.

Baxter State Park is open May 15–November 1 and December 1–March 31. During the summer season, the park's Togue Pond Gate is open 6 A.M.–10 P.M.—though it may open at 5 A.M. at the discretion of the park director; the Matagamon Gate is open 6 A.M.–10 P.M. The road is not maintained to the trailhead in winter, but it can be skied. GPS Coordinates: 45.8740 N, 68.9660 W

Contact: Baxter State Park, 64 Balsam Dr., Millinocket, ME 04462-2190, 207/723-5140, www.baxterstateparkauthority.com.

11 LITTLE ABOL FALLS

1.6 mi/1 hr

In southern Baxter State Park

Leaving from the Abol Campground in the shadow of Katahdin's soaring south wall, this easy walk along a path of packed dirt and gravel ascends gently 0.8 mile to a scenic waterfall on a branch of Abol Stream. With a shear drop of 15 feet, the fall forms a pleasant pool—and a popular swimming hole. Nearby campers and day hikers on their way back down the mountain flock to the cooling waters, especially on hot summer days. If you want some solitude at the falls, try going in the early morning.

From the Abol Campground parking area, walk up the campground road. The Little Abol Falls Trail begins at the upper end of the campground, between lean-tos #8 and #10. Follow the well-worn path and take in views of the southwest side of Katahdin, including Abol Slide. At 0.8 mile, reach the stream and follow alongside it as the water makes a sudden drop to the pool below. The trail takes you down to the pool. Return the way you came.

User Groups: Hikers only. No wheelchair facilities. Bikes, dogs, and horses are prohibited.

Permits: No permits required. An entrance fee of $13 per vehicle is charged at the gatehouse, but vehicles bearing Maine registration can enter at no charge.

Maps: A waterproof trail map of Baxter State Park is available from the Appalachian Mountain Club (Rangeley–Stratton/Baxter State Park–Katahdin map, $7.95). For a topographic map, ask the USGS for Mount Katahdin and Katahdin Lake.

Directions: From Millinocket, head west on Central Street/Route 11/Route 157 toward State Street. Turn right at Katahdin Avenue and follow briefly before turning left at Bates Street. This street becomes Millinocket Road. After 7.4 miles, bear right at the fork for Baxter Park Road. Follow another 8.4 miles before reaching the park's Togue Pond gate. Just beyond the gatehouse, take the right fork on the gravel Tote Road (the park's perimeter road) and drive 5.7 miles to Abol Campground and day-use parking on the left, opposite the campground entrance.

Baxter State Park is open May 15–November 1 and December 1–March 31. During the summer season, the park's Togue Pond Gate is open 6 A.M.–10 P.M.—though it may open at 5 A.M. at the discretion of the park director; the Matagamon Gate is open 6 A.M.–10 P.M. The road is not maintained to the trailhead in winter, but it can be skied.

GPS Coordinates: 45.8740 N, 68.9616 W

Contact: Baxter State Park, 64 Balsam Dr., Millinocket, ME 04462-2190, 207/723-5140, www.baxterstateparkauthority.com.

12 KATAHDIN: HUNT TRAIL

10 mi/8 hr

In southern Baxter State Park

Ascending the Katahdin massif (5,267 ft.) from the southwest, the rugged Hunt Trail gains 4,100 feet in elevation from its trailhead near Katahdin Stream Campground, much of it above timberline. The final stretch of the Appalachian Trail for northbound through-hikers on their way to the mountain's Baxter Peak summit, the Hunt Trail ends the epic 2,174-mile journey with a number of outstanding features: waterfalls, boulder fields, an expansive tableland, almost limitless views, and the chance to stand atop the highest spot in Maine. This was the same trail 19th century naturalist Henry David Thoreau used on his climb to Katahdin (described in his book, *The Maine Woods*). Thoreau wrote about the solitude of his ascent, but you probably won't be able to do the same. From the start of the warm weather hiking season in July until its end on October 15, the Hunt Trail is one of the most heavily trafficked in the whole of Baxter.

Pick up the white-blazed Hunt Trail at the

northeast end of Katahdin Stream Campground. Running parallel to Katahdin Stream for the first mile, the climb here is gradual and mainly forest covered. At 2.8 miles from the campground, the trail abruptly breaks out above the trees and the ascent quickly steepens. Around the three-mile mark, iron rungs drilled into the stone help you scale a short, vertical rock face.

Topping the rocky, open ridge crest, the trail reaches the Tableland, a mile-wide plateau at about 4,500 feet, a tundra littered with rocks. The trail passes Thoreau Spring near the Abol Trail junction before finally ascending to the main summit, panoramic Baxter Peak. A large sign marks the Appalachian Trail's northern terminus. Some 2,000 feet below is the blue dot of Chimney Pond. To the right (east) is the serrated crest of the Knife Edge, and to the north lie Hamlin Peak, the Howe Peaks, and the vast Baxter Park wilderness. Descend the same way you came up.

User Groups: Hikers only. No wheelchair facilities. Bikes, dogs, and horses are prohibited. This trail should not be attempted in winter except by hikers experienced in mountaineering and prepared for severe winter weather; not suitable for skis.

Permits: No permits required. An entrance fee of $13 per vehicle is charged at the gatehouse, but vehicles bearing Maine registration can enter at no charge.

Maps: A waterproof trail map of Baxter State Park is available from the Appalachian Mountain Club (Rangeley–Stratton/Baxter State Park–Katahdin map, $7.95). For a topographic map, ask the USGS for Mount Katahdin and Katahdin Lake.

Directions: From Millinocket, head west on Central Street/Route 11/Route 157 toward State Street. Turn right at Katahdin Avenue and follow briefly before turning left at Bates Street. This street becomes Millinocket Road. After 7.4 miles, bear right at the fork for Baxter Park Road. Follow another 8.4 miles before reaching the park's Togue Pond gate. Just beyond the gatehouse, take the right fork on the gravel Tote Road (the park's perimeter road) and drive eight miles to Katahdin Stream Campground. Turn right onto the campground road and continue 0.1 mile to the day-use parking area.

Baxter State Park is open May 15–November 1 and December 1–March 31. During the summer season, the park's Togue Pond Gate is open 6 A.M.–10 P.M.—though it may open at 5 A.M. at the discretion of the park director; the Matagamon Gate is open 6 A.M.–10 P.M. The road is not maintained to the trailhead in winter, but it can be skied.

GPS Coordinates: 45.8873 N, 68.9983 W

Contact: Baxter State Park, 64 Balsam Dr., Millinocket, ME 04462-2190, 207/723-5140, www.baxterstateparkauthority.com.

13 KATAHDIN STREAM FALLS

2.4 mi/1.5 hr ╠╣1 ▲8

in southern Baxter State Park

A popular stopping off point for hikers ascending (and descending) Katahdin along the Hunt Trail, Katahdin Stream Falls tumbles about 50 feet and is visible from the trail after an easy walk of just over a mile up from the Hunt trailhead. Leaving the Katahdin Stream Campground parking area, follow the white blazes of the Hunt Trail, which is the Appalachian Trail's final stretch. It ascends easily through the woods. After passing a junction with the Owl Trail at the one-mile mark, continue 0.1 mile and cross on a wooden bridge over Katahdin Stream. Just 0.1 mile farther, a short spur trail leads to the waterfall. Enjoy the cascading spray and head back the way you came.

User Groups: Hikers only. No wheelchair facilities. Bikes, dogs, and horses are prohibited. This trail should not be attempted in winter except by hikers experienced in mountaineering and prepared for severe winter weather; not suitable for skis.

Permits: No permits required. An entrance fee of $13 per vehicle is charged at the gatehouse, but vehicles bearing Maine registration can enter at no charge.

Maps: A waterproof trail map of Baxter State Park is available from the Appalachian Mountain Club (Rangeley–Stratton/Baxter State Park–Katahdin map, $7.95). For a topographic map, ask the USGS for Mount Katahdin and Katahdin Lake.

Directions: From Millinocket, head west on Central Street/Route 11/Route 157 toward State Street. Turn right at Katahdin Avenue and follow briefly before turning left at Bates Street. This street becomes Millinocket Road. After 7.4 miles, bear right at the fork for Baxter Park Road. Follow another 8.4 miles before reaching the park's Togue Pond gate. Just beyond the gatehouse, take the right fork on the gravel Tote Road (the park's perimeter road) and drive eight miles to Katahdin Stream Campground. Turn right onto the campground road and continue 0.1 mile to the day-use parking area.

Baxter State Park is open May 15–November 1 and December 1–March 31. During the summer season, the park's Togue Pond Gate is open 6 A.M.–10 P.M.—though it may open at 5 A.M. at the discretion of the park director; the Matagamon Gate is open 6 A.M.–10 P.M. The road is not maintained to the trailhead in winter, but it can be skied.

GPS Coordinates: 45.8873 N, 68.9983 W

Contact: Baxter State Park, 64 Balsam Dr., Millinocket, ME 04462-2190, 207/723-5140, www.baxterstateparkauthority.com.

14 THE OWL

6 mi/6 hr　　　　　　🏃5 ⛰10

in southern Baxter State Park

One of the most arduous hikes in Baxter State Park and one of its best-kept secrets, this six-mile round-tripper climbs some 2,600 feet to the 3,736-foot summit of the Owl, visible from the Hunt Trail/Appalachian Trail ridge on neighboring Katahdin.

From the day-use parking area at Katahdin Stream Campground, follow the white blazes of the Hunt Trail, the Appalachian Trail's final stretch, and ascend easily through the woods. After one mile, turn left at the sign for the Owl Trail, and if your timing is right, you're in for a sweet treat—the trail here is lined with ripe blueberries in late August and early September. In less than a mile from the Hunt Trail, cross a boulder field. Continue on and about 0.2 mile below the summit, you emerge onto an open ledge with a great view down into the Katahdin Stream ravine and across to Katahdin. Some hikers may want to turn around from here because the trail grows increasingly difficult and exposed.

If you decide to persevere, scramble up rocks to a second ledge, where a boulder perches at the brink of a precipice (is this a watchful owl perched on its branch?). After another short scramble, you reach the level shoulder of the Owl. The trail follows the crest of that narrow ridge, ducking briefly through a subalpine forest and ascending slightly to the bare ledges at the summit, where there are sweeping views in every direction. An example of Baxter's famed striped forest (alternating waves of old and new growth forest) is visible to the west. Katahdin dominates the skyline to the east; the Northwest Plateau lies to the northeast; the Brothers, Coe, and O-J-I to the west; and the wilderness lakes along the Appalachian Trail to the south. Descend along the same route.

User Groups: Hikers only. No wheelchair facilities. Bikes, dogs, and horses are prohibited. This trail should not be attempted in winter except by hikers experienced in mountaineering and prepared for severe winter weather; not suitable for skis.

Permits: No permits required. An entrance fee of $13 per vehicle is charged at the gatehouse, but vehicles bearing Maine registration can enter at no charge.

Maps: A waterproof trail map of Baxter State Park is available from the Appalachian

Mountain Club (Rangeley–Stratton/Baxter State Park–Katahdin map, $7.95). For topographic area maps, request Doubletop Mountain and Mount Katahdin from the USGS.

Directions: From Millinocket, head west on Central Street/Route 11/Route 157 toward State Street. Turn right at Katahdin Avenue and follow briefly before turning left at Bates Street. This street becomes Millinocket Road. After 7.4 miles, bear right at the fork for Baxter Park Road. Follow another 8.4 miles before reaching the park's Togue Pond gate. Just beyond the gatehouse, take the right fork on the gravel Tote Road (the park's perimeter road) and drive eight miles to Katahdin Stream Campground. Turn right onto the campground road and continue 0.1 mile to the day-use parking area.

Baxter State Park is open May 15–November 1 and December 1–March 31. During the summer season, the park's Togue Pond Gate is open 6 A.M.–10 P.M.—though it may open at 5 A.M. at the discretion of the park director; the Matagamon Gate is open 6 A.M.–10 P.M. The road is not maintained to the trailhead in winter, but it can be skied.

GPS Coordinates: 45.8873 N, 68.9983 W

Contact: Baxter State Park, 64 Balsam Dr., Millinocket, ME 04462-2190, 207/723-5140, www.baxterstateparkauthority.com.

🔢 NORTH BROTHER
9.0 mi/6 hr

in southern Baxter State Park

At 4,143 feet, Maine's seventh-highest mountain has a fairly extensive summit area above the tree line and the excellent views from the peak encompass Katahdin to the southeast, the remote Northwest Plateau and Basin to the east, Fort and Traveler mountains to the north, Doubletop to the west, and the wild, trail-less area known as the Klondike to the immediate south. The hike gains about 2,900 feet in elevation.

From the Slide Dam Picnic Area parking lot, follow the gently ascending Marston Trail almost due west for 1.2 miles. Reaching a trail junction, the Marston Trail turns sharply left (north) and continues on to a small pond (at 2.2 miles from the trailhead). Here, the climb becomes suddenly steep and relentless as you ascend a basin wall, a strenuous 0.7 mile. At the top of the basin, the trail flattens out for the next 0.8 mile before dropping into a sag between North and South Brother and reaching another junction. To the right (south) is the summit trail for South Brother (3,930 feet). To reach the summit of North Brother, turn left and climb another 0.8 mile. A good example of Baxter's famous striped forest (alternating waves of old and new growth forest) is visible between South and North Brother. Return the same way you hiked up.

Special note: You can combine this hike with the hike up Mount Coe, and bag South Brother as well, in a loop of 9.4 miles. The best route is to ascend the Mount Coe slide, hitting Coe first, then continuing on the Mount Coe Trail to South Brother, and finally bagging North Brother, then descending the Marston Trail. (See the *Mount Coe* listing in this chapter.)

User Groups: Hikers only. No wheelchair facilities. Bikes, dogs, and horses are prohibited. This trail should not be attempted in winter except by hikers experienced in mountaineering and prepared for severe winter weather; not suitable for skis.

Permits: No permits required. An entrance fee of $13 per vehicle is charged at the gatehouse, but vehicles bearing Maine registration can enter at no charge.

Maps: A waterproof trail map of Baxter State Park is available from the Appalachian Mountain Club (Rangeley–Stratton/Baxter State Park–Katahdin map, $7.95). For topographic area maps, request Doubletop Mountain and Mount Katahdin from the USGS.

Directions: From Millinocket, head west on Central Street/Route 11/Route 157 toward State Street. Turn right at Katahdin Avenue and follow briefly before turning left at Bates Street. This street becomes Millinocket Road. After 7.4 miles, bear right at the fork for Baxter Park Road. Follow another 8.4 miles before reaching the park's Togue Pond gate. Just beyond the gatehouse, take the gravel Tote Road's left fork and drive 13.5 miles to a parking area on the right for the Marston Trail.

Baxter State Park is open May 15–November 1 and December 1–March 31. During the summer season, the park's Togue Pond Gate is open 6 A.M.–10 P.M.—though it may open at 5 A.M. at the discretion of the park director; the Matagamon Gate is open 6 A.M.–10 P.M. The road is not maintained to the trailhead in winter, but it can be skied.

GPS Coordinates: 45.9406 N, 69.0433 W

Contact: Baxter State Park, 64 Balsam Dr., Millinocket, ME 04462-2190, 207/723-5140, www.baxterstateparkauthority.com.

16 MOUNT COE
6.6 mi/6 hr
🏃5 ⛰9

in southern Baxter State Park

Mount Coe's 3,764-foot summit has a sweeping view of the southern end of Baxter State Park, including east over the trail-less wilderness area of the Klondike and on toward Katahdin and the Northwest Plateau. This 6.6-mile out-and-back hike ascends about 2,500 feet.

From the Slide Dam Picnic Area parking lot, follow the Marston Trail for 1.2 miles to a trail junction. Bear right here onto the Mount Coe Trail. It ascends easily at first, reaching the foot of the Mount Coe rockslide, still in the forest, within a quarter of a mile. The trail emerges about a mile farther onto the open, broad scar of the slide, and for the next half mile climbs the slide's steep slabs and loose stone; this section becomes treacherous when wet, with the potential for injurious falls. Watch closely for the blazes and rock cairns because the trail zigzags several times across the slide.

Near the top of the slide, a side trail—easy to overlook—branches right, leading 0.7 mile to the Mount O-J-I summit. This hike continues straight up the slide, enters the scrub forest, and reaches the Mount Coe summit 3.3 miles from the Marston trailhead. This hike descends the same way you came.

User Groups: Hikers only. No wheelchair facilities. Bikes, dogs, and horses are prohibited. This trail should not be attempted in winter except by hikers experienced in mountaineering and prepared for severe winter weather, and is not suitable for skis.

Permits: No permits required. An entrance fee of $13 per vehicle is charged at the gatehouse, but vehicles bearing Maine registration can enter at no charge.

Maps: A waterproof trail map of Baxter State Park is available from the Appalachian Mountain Club (Rangeley–Stratton/Baxter State Park–Katahdin map, $7.95). For topographic area maps, request Doubletop Mountain and Mount Katahdin from the USGS.

Directions: From Millinocket, head west on Central Street/Route 11/Route 157 toward State Street. Turn right at Katahdin Avenue and follow briefly before turning left at Bates Street. This street becomes Millinocket Road. After 7.4 miles, bear right at the fork for Baxter Park Road. Follow another 8.4 miles before reaching the park's Togue Pond gate. Just beyond the gatehouse, take the gravel Tote Road's left fork and drive 13.5 miles to a parking area on the right for the Marston Trail.

Baxter State Park is open May 15–November 1 and December 1–March 31. During the summer season, the park's Togue Pond Gate is open 6 A.M.–10 P.M.—though it may open at 5 A.M. at the discretion of the park director; the Matagamon Gate is open 6 A.M.–10 P.M. The road is not maintained to the trailhead in winter, but it can be skied.

GPS Coordinates: 45.9406 N, 69.0433 W

Contact: Baxter State Park, 64 Balsam Dr., Millinocket, ME 04462-2190, 207/723-5140, www.baxterstateparkauthority.com.

17 MOUNT O-J-I
5.8 mi/6 hr ♘5 ◮9

in southern Baxter State Park

O-J-I takes its name from the shapes of three slides that—when seen from the southwest—resemble those letters (although the slides have expanded and the letters have become obscured in recent decades). This 5.8-mile loop up 3,410-foot Mount O-J-I is a very strenuous hike. It climbs about 2,300 feet, but more significantly, involves fairly serious scrambling. The South Slide trail to the summit is steep, with lots of loose rock and slabs that are hazardous when wet. Hiking time can vary greatly depending upon your comfort level on exposed rock. But you enjoy extensive views from the slides to the west and south, and excellent views from points near the summit.

From the Foster Field parking area, walk the road toward Foster Field for about 50 feet and turn right onto the South Slide Trail. For the first 0.4 mile the terrain is flat, crossing wet areas. At 1.8 miles from the trailhead, the slide begins. Ascend steeply and scramble your way up the loose rock, carefully following the trail's cairns and blue blazes. At 2.4 miles, the trail reaches the head of the slide and reenters the woods for a more gradual climb. Pass a trail junction at 2.7 miles (you can follow the O-J-I Link trail here to use neighboring Mount Coe as an alternate descent route). Continue on 0.1 mile and pass another trail junction (a short spur to a scenic overlook). At 2.9 miles from the trailhead, reach the summit of O-J-I, with excellent views of the wild Klondike Basin area of Baxter, Mount Coe, and the west side of Katahdin. Return the way you came.

User Groups: Hikers only. No wheelchair facilities. Bikes, dogs, and horses are prohibited. This trail should not be attempted in winter except by hikers experienced in mountaineering and prepared for severe winter weather; not suitable for skis.

Permits: No permits required. An entrance fee

of $13 per vehicle is charged at the gatehouse, but vehicles bearing Maine registration can enter at no charge.

Maps: A waterproof trail map of Baxter State Park is available from the Appalachian Mountain Club (Rangeley–Stratton/Baxter State Park–Katahdin map, $7.95). For topographic area maps, request Doubletop Mountain and Mount Katahdin from the USGS.

Directions: From Millinocket, head west on Central Street/Route 11/Route 157 toward State Street. Turn right at Katahdin Avenue and follow briefly before turning left at Bates Street. This street becomes Millinocket Road. After 7.4 miles, bear right at the fork for Baxter Park Road. Follow another 8.4 miles before reaching the park's Togue Pond gate. Just beyond the gatehouse, take the gravel Tote Road's left fork and drive 10.5 miles to a day-use parking area, just before Foster Field.

Baxter State Park is open May 15–November 1 and December 1–March 31. During the summer season, the park's Togue Pond Gate is open 6 A.M.–10 P.M.—though it may open at 5 A.M. at the discretion of the park director; the Matagamon Gate is open 6 A.M.–10 P.M. The road is not maintained to the trailhead in winter, but it can be skied.

GPS Coordinates: 45.9036 N, 69.0372 W

Contact: Baxter State Park, 64 Balsam Dr., Millinocket, ME 04462-2190, 207/723-5140, www.baxterstateparkauthority.com.

18 DOUBLETOP MOUNTAIN
6 mi/5.5 hr ♘4 ◮10

in southern Baxter State Park

Measuring 3,488 feet, Doubletop Mountain's distinctive high ridge stands out prominently from various points around Baxter State Park's south end, rising like an upturned ax blade above the narrow valley of Nesowadnehunk Stream. Much of the quarter mile of ridge connecting the north and south peaks lies above the tree line, affording outstanding views of

Katahdin to the east, the cluster of peaks immediately north that include the Brothers, Coe, and O-J-I, and the wilderness lakes to the south. This six-mile hike ascends about 2,200 feet.

From the Nesowadnehunk Campground parking area, follow the road into the campground and past campsites. At half a mile in, the road ends at the Doubletop trailhead. The trail is flat until crossing a stream at 1.2 miles. Here begins a very steep climb of almost two miles, leveling out briefly on the mountain's north shoulder, and then ascending again. After climbing a short iron ladder, you emerge above the forest, a few steps from the North Peak of Doubletop (3,488 ft.). The trail drops off that summit to the west, then turns south and follows the ridge for 0.2 mile to the lower South Peak. Return the same way you hiked up.

User Groups: Hikers only. No wheelchair facilities. Bikes, dogs, and horses are prohibited. This trail should not be attempted in winter except by hikers experienced in mountaineering and prepared for severe winter weather; not suitable for skis.

Permits: No permits required. An entrance fee of $13 per vehicle is charged at the gatehouse, but vehicles bearing Maine registration can enter at no charge.

Maps: A waterproof trail map of Baxter State Park is available from the Appalachian Mountain Club (Rangeley–Stratton/Baxter State Park–Katahdin map, $7.95). For topographic area maps, request Doubletop Mountain and Mount Katahdin from the USGS.

Directions: From Millinocket, head west on Central Street/Route 11/Route 157 toward State Street. Turn right at Katahdin Avenue and follow briefly before turning left at Bates Street. This street becomes Millinocket Road. After 7.4 miles, bear right at the fork for Baxter Park Road. Follow another 8.4 miles before reaching the park's Togue Pond gate. Just beyond the gatehouse, take the gravel Tote Road's left fork and drive 16.9 miles, then turn left into the Nesowadnehunk Field Campground. Drive 0.3 mile to the parking area on the right.

Baxter State Park is open May 15–November 1 and from December 1–March 31. During the summer season, the park's Togue Pond Gate is open 6 A.M.–10 P.M.—though it may open at 5 A.M. at the discretion of the park director; the Matagamon Gate is open 6 A.M.–10 P.M. The road is not maintained to the trailhead in winter, but it can be skied. GPS Coordinates: 45.9736 N, 69.0755 W

Contact: Baxter State Park, 64 Balsam Dr., Millinocket, ME 04462-2190, 207/723-5140, www.baxterstateparkauthority.com.

19 KIDNEY POND LOOP
3.1 mi/1.5 hr 👫1 ⛺8

in southern Baxter State Park

BEST (

This easy 3.1-mile loop around Kidney Pond offers a chance to see moose and pondlife, and comes with good views across the pond toward Katahdin, Doubletop, and O-J-I. Side paths lead to such scenic viewing spots as the Colt's Point peninsula; other paths radiate outward from the loop trail, leading the way to Rocky Pond and other nearby ponds. This is the perfect spot for a family outing to Baxter: Summertime nature programs for kids (run by park staff) often take place in and around the Kidney Pond area.

From the rear of the parking area for Kidney Pond Campground, pick up the trailhead at a sign for the Kidney Pond Loop. The trail follows the pond's shore at first, then skirts wide of it into the woods at its southern end. Pass through mixed forest (a great place to find and identify animal tracks), follow and cross a shallow stream, and eventually reach the campground road. Turn left on the road and walk the quarter mile back to the parking area.

User Groups: Hikers only. No wheelchair facilities. Bikes, dogs, and horses are prohibited.

Permits: No permits required. An entrance fee

Moose are a common sight in Maine's North Woods.

of $13 per vehicle is charged at the gatehouse, but vehicles bearing Maine registration can enter at no charge.

Maps: A waterproof trail map of Baxter State Park is available from the Appalachian Mountain Club (Rangeley–Stratton/Baxter State Park–Katahdin map, $7.95). For topographic area maps, request Doubletop Mountain from the USGS.

Directions: From Millinocket, head west on Central Street/Route 11/Route 157 toward State Street. Turn right at Katahdin Avenue and follow briefly before turning left at Bates Street. This street becomes Millinocket Road. After 7.4 miles, bear right at the fork for Baxter Park Road. Follow another 8.4 miles before reaching the park's Togue Pond gate. Just beyond the gatehouse, take the dirt perimeter road's left fork and drive 10.6 miles, then turn left at a sign for Kidney Pond Camps. Drive 1.1 miles to the parking area.

Baxter State Park is open May 15–November 1 and December 1–March 31. During the summer season, the park's Togue Pond Gate is open 6 A.M.–10 P.M.—though it may open at 5 A.M. at the discretion of the park director; the Matagamon Gate is open 6 A.M.–10 P.M. The road is not maintained to the trailhead in winter, but it can be skied.
GPS Coordinates: 45.8929 N, 69.0482 W
Contact: Baxter State Park, 64 Balsam Dr., Millinocket, ME 04462-2190, 207/723-5140, www.baxterstateparkauthority.com.

20 POLLYWOG GORGE
3.8 mi/2.5 hr   👣2 ⛰8

southwest of Baxter State Park

What's to see in the North Woods outside Baxter State Park? This pleasant hike makes a 3.8-mile loop through scenic Pollywog Gorge, a small ledge high above the rushing waters of Pollywog Stream. Starting and finishing on a 1.2-mile stretch of logging road within the 100-Mile Wilderness, this hike also follows parts of the Appalachian Trail (AT).

From the roadside parking just before the bridge over Pollywog Stream, turn left (southbound) on the AT and follow it one mile to a side path leading to the gorge overlook. Continue south on the AT through woods and around Crescent Pond to the logging road, 2.6 miles from the hike's start. Turn left and follow the road 1.2 miles back to the bridge.

The Rainbow Stream lean-to is located 2.4 miles north on the AT from the Pollywog Stream bridge (not along this hike). It's legal to camp anywhere along the AT in the 100-Mile Wilderness; low-impact camping is encouraged.

User Groups: Hikers only. No wheelchair facilities. Dogs are discouraged along the Appalachian Trail in Maine. Bikes and horses are prohibited. This trail should not be attempted in winter except by hikers prepared for severe winter weather, and is not suitable for skis.

Permits: No permits required.

Maps: For a trail map, refer to map 1 in the *Map and Guide to the Appalachian Trail in Maine,* a set of seven maps and a guidebook for $25.00 from the Maine Appalachian Trail Club. For a topographic area map, request Rainbow Lake West from the USGS.

Directions: From the junction of Routes 11 and 157 in Millinocket, head south on Route 11 for 15.5 miles. Cross over Bear Brook and turn west onto private, gravel Jo-Mary Road, which isn't passable at certain times of year due to snow or muddy conditions. In 0.2 mile, pass through a gate and pay a vehicle toll. Continue six miles from the gate and bear right at a sign for the Appalachian Trail. Follow that road another 20.2 miles (ignoring unimproved roads diverging from it) to where the AT crosses Pollywog Stream on a bridge; park at the roadside.

GPS Coordinates: 45.7793 N, 69.1725 W

Contact: Maine Appalachian Trail Club, P.O. Box 283, Augusta, ME 04332-0283, www.matc.org.

21 100-MILE WILDERNESS
99.4 mi one-way/9-10 days

👣5 ⛰10

between Monson and Baxter State Park

BEST (

From its starting point just north of Monson on Route 15 to where it ends at the West Branch of the Penobscot River outside Baxter State Park's southern boundary, the 100-Mile Wilderness stretch of the Appalachian Trail runs for 99.4 miles without crossing a paved or public road. (The trail is, however, bisected by a number of private logging roads.) A land of dense forest, wandering streams, and rugged hills, and home to moose, bears, and countless other species of northern wildlife, the Wilderness still constitutes one of the most remote backpacking experiences possible in New England. It's busiest in August and early September when the weather is warm and drier, the mosquitoes have dissipated somewhat, and Appalachian Trail through-hikers arrive on the last long leg of their journey towards Katahdin. Hit the trail in July or early October and you may find yourself making the 99.4-mile trek in almost complete solitude.

The number of days spent on this trail can vary greatly. Generally, the southern half, below Crawford Pond, is more mountainous and rugged; and from Crawford north the trail covers easier, flatter terrain around several vast wilderness lakes. If you do plan to hike the entire 99.4-mile stretch, bringing along water filtration/purification equipment is a

fording the East Branch of Pleasant River at mile 47 of the 100-Mile Wilderness

© PETE LORD

must. The trail is well-marked with the white blazes of the Appalachian Trail (AT) and there are signs at many junctions.

From the parking turnout area north of Monson on Route 15 (mile 0), the AT enters the woods at a well-marked trail sign. Traversing relatively easy terrain past a number of small ponds, the trail soon reaches one of the many lean-tos scattered along the trail. Here, Leeman Brook lean-to (mile 3.0), sleeps six and sits above a small gorge. Continuing north, the trail crosses a logging road (at mile 4.2; passing logging trucks have the right of way on all logging roads, so show caution) and then pushes on to reach the top of 60-foot Little Wilson Falls (mile 6.6), one of the highest waterfalls along the AT. The trail turns sharply right, following the rim of the long, deep gorge below the falls, then descends steeply, eventually fording Little Wilson Stream (mile 6.8) with a good view upstream into the gorge. Turn left onto a gravel logging road (mile 7.2) and follow it for 100 yards, and then turn right into the woods. At the Big Wilson logging road (mile 9.1), turn left, follow it for 0.6 mile; then turn right off the road (mile 9.7) and ford Big Wilson Stream, which can be difficult in high water. A bridge across the stream is available 1.5 miles downstream. After crossing the bridge, take the unmarked path 1.5 miles back upstream to rejoin the AT. At mile 10, cross the Canadian Pacific Railroad line.

Less than a half mile from the railroad

right-of-way, a short side path leads right to the Wilson Valley lean-to (mile 10.4), which sleeps six; there is water at a nearby spring. The trail then continues on for the next five miles, fording Wilbur Brook (mile 13.6) and Vaughn Stream (mile 13.7) above a spectacular 20-foot waterfall that drops into a broad pool. At a logging road (mile 14.2), turn right and walk 100 yards and then left again into the woods. Ford Long Pond Stream (mile 14.3), walk alongside narrow pools and flumes of smooth rock, and then reach a short side path at 15 miles that leads left to Slugundy Gorge, a scenic gorge and falls. Just beyond, another side path leads left 150 yards to the Long Pond Stream lean-to, which sleeps eight; get water from the nearby brook.

Beyond the shelter, the AT begins the steep climb of Barren Mountain. At mile 16.2, a side path leads to the right about 250 feet to the top of the Barren Slide, from which there are excellent views south of Lake Onawa and Borestone Mountain. Following the ridge, the trail reaches the 2,670-foot summit of Barren Mountain (mile 18.2), which offers sweeping views, particularly south and west; also here is an abandoned fire tower. Dropping back into the woods, you pass a side trail (mile 19.1) leading right 0.3 mile to the beautiful tarn called Cloud Pond and a nearby lean-to; water can be obtained from a spring or the pond.

Continuing along the Barren-Chairback Ridge, the trail bounces over rugged terrain, passing over the wooded 2,383-foot summit of Fourth Mountain (mile 21.2) and a side path leading right 0.2 mile to West Chairback Pond (mile 24.3). Just beyond that path, the AT crosses a good stream where you may want to load up on water if you're planning to stay at the Chairback Gap lean-to, where the spring may run dry in late summer. The trail climbs steeply over Columbus Mountain, then drops into Chairback Gap, passing in front of the lean-to there; the spring is about 200 yards downhill along the trail. The trail then ascends to the top of 2,219-foot Chairback Mountain (mile 26.5), traversing its long, open crest with

excellent views west and north. At the end of the ridge, the trail descends a very steep slope (mile 26.6) of loose talus, trending left near its bottom. It passes over open ledges (mile 26.9) with views back to Chairback Mountain. At mile 29.9, cross a wide logging road; half a mile to the right (east) is a parking area heavily used by day visitors to Gulf Hagas. The road continues east for 7.1 miles to the Katahdin Iron Works Museum.

The AT passes through woods onward to the West Branch of Pleasant River (mile 30.4), a wide channel that might be knee-deep during an August trip, but could be dangerous at high water. (Before fording the river, you will notice a blue-blazed trail; this leads back to the parking area on the logging road.) After crossing the river, the AT follows easy ground through a forest of tall white pines; a short side path (mile 30.7) leads right to the Hermitage, a stand of white pines up to 130 feet tall. At mile 32, the AT hooks right, and a blue-blazed trail leads straight ahead to the 5.2-mile loop through Gulf Hagas, one of the most scenic areas along the AT's Maine corridor and a very worthwhile detour if you have the time (see the *Gulf Hagas* listing in this chapter). The AT ascends steadily northward for 4.2 miles, following Gulf Hagas Brook to the Carl A. Newhall lean-to and tent sites; the lean-to, accessed by a short side path off the AT (mile 35.9), sleeps six, and water is available from the brook. Climbing steeply, the trail passes over the 2,683-foot summit of Gulf Hagas Mountain (mile 36.8), where there are limited views to the west from just north of the true summit, and then descends to the Sidney Tappen Campsite (mile 37.7) for tents only; a nearby spring provides water. Continue north along the arduous ridge, over 3,178-foot West Peak (mile 38.4), with limited views, and the wooded summit of 3,244-foot Hay Mountain (mile 40.0).

At mile 40.6, the White Brook Trail departs to the right (east), descending 1.9 miles to logging roads that eventually link with the road to Katahdin Iron Works. The AT then climbs to the highest point on the ridge and one of the finest views along the 100-Mile Wilderness, the 3,654-foot summit of White Cap Mountain (mile 41.7), where you get your first view on this hike of Mount Katahdin to the north. White Cap is the last big peak in the 100-Mile Wilderness. Descending north off White Cap and passing an open ledge with another good view toward Katahdin (mile 42.5), the trail reaches the Logan Brook lean-to (mile 43.1), which sleeps six. Cross a gravel road (mile 44.7) to reach another lean-to (mile 46.8). The trail fords the East Branch of Pleasant River (mile 47.0), which could be difficult at high water, and then climbs over 2,017-foot Little Boardman Mountain (mile 50.2).

Descending easily, the AT crosses the dirt Kokadjo-B Pond Road (mile 51.6), enters the woods, and soon reaches the east shore of Crawford Pond (mile 51.7). Heading slightly northward along an old woods road, the AT reaches a side path (mile 54.8) leading 150 feet to the right to the Cooper Brook Falls lean-to and the spectacular cascades along Cooper Brook. Continuing along, the trail crosses the dirt Jo-Mary Road (mile 58.5) beside a bridge over Cooper Brook. To reach Route 11, turn right (east) and follow Jo-Mary Road for 12 miles. To keep on the AT, cross the road and reenter the woods.

Now passing through mainly flat, easy terrain, the AT crosses a gravel road (mile 61.4), fords several streams in succession (mile 61.5), crosses another old logging road (mile 62.0), and reaches a short side path (mile 62.7), veering right to the Antlers Campsite, a tenting area set amid red pines on a land point jutting into vast Lower Jo-Mary Lake. From that junction, the AT hooks left and swings around the lake's west shore to a junction with the Potaywadjo Ridge Trail (mile 64.2), which leads left. Ascend steadily for one mile to broad, open ledges on Potaywadjo Ridge, with sweeping views of the lakes and mountains to the south and east. This is one of the finest viewpoints in the northern half of

the 100-Mile Wilderness and a great place for picking blueberries in late August. From that junction, the AT ascends the wooded end of the ridge and then drops to the Potaywadjo Spring lean-to (mile 66.2), which sleeps six. Following easy terrain again, the AT passes a junction with a side path (mile 66.8) leading a short distance to the shore of Pemadumcook Lake, where you get an excellent view across the water to Katahdin. Cross Deer Brook (mile 68.0), an old logging road (mile 68.8), and then ford a tributary of Nahmakanta Stream (mile 68.9). A high-water bypass trail 0.2 mile long diverges from the AT (mile 69.3) and then rejoins it (mile 69.4). At mile 70, you ford Tumbledown Dick Stream.

The AT parallels Nahmakanta Stream, where footing grows difficult over many rocks and roots, and then crosses a gravel road (mile 73.4); to reach Route 11, you would turn left (southwest) and continue 24 miles on this gravel road to the Jo-Mary Road. The AT crosses the gravel road and reenters the woods. At mile 73.8, the AT reaches the south shore of Nahmakanta Lake near a short side path leading to a gravel beach. It follows the lakeshore, skirting into the woods and out onto the rocky shore to a short side path (mile 76.0) leading right to a sandy beach; the path emerges at one end of the beach, near a small spring. From here, the AT crosses Wadleigh Stream (mile 76.3) and then reaches the Wadleigh Stream lean-to (mile 76.4), which sleeps six; the nearby stream provides water. The trail then makes a steep ascent up Nesuntabunt Mountain; from its north summit (mile 78.3), a short side path leads to an open ledge with an excellent view from high above Nahmakanta Lake toward Katahdin. Descending somewhat more moderately off Nesuntabunt, the AT crosses a logging road (mile 79.5); to the north, it's 1.2 miles to Pollywog Bridge, and to the south it's 25.2 miles to Route 11. This hike crosses the logging road and reenters the woods.

After circling Crescent Pond (mile 80.1), the AT passes a short side path (mile 81.1) leading left to a rather exposed ledge high above Pollywog Gorge. It then parallels Pollywog Stream to a logging road (mile 82.1); to reach Route 11, you would turn south and follow the road 26.4 miles. The AT turns left and crosses the stream on a bridge. Walk past a dirt road branching right and reenter the woods to the right. The trail follows a picturesque gorge along Rainbow Stream for about two miles and then reaches the Rainbow Stream lean-to (mile 84.5), which sleeps six; water is available from the stream. From here, easy terrain leads to a small clearing (mile 89.8); to the right, a short path leads to tent sites at the Rainbow Spring Campsite, and to the left, it's just a short walk to the spring and Rainbow Lake. Continuing along the big lake's shore, the AT reaches the Rainbow Mountain Trail at mile 90, which bears right and climbs a fairly easy 1.1 miles to the bare summit of Rainbow Mountain with excellent views, especially toward Katahdin.

The AT continues to the east end of Rainbow Lake (mile 91.7), passes a side path (mile 91.8) leading right 0.1 mile to Little Beaver Pond and 0.4 mile to Big Beaver Pond, and then ascends to Rainbow Ledges (mile 93.5); from various points along the ledges you get long views south and northeast to Katahdin. Descending easily, the AT fords Hurd Brook (mile 96.0), which can be difficult when the water is high, and reaches the Hurd Brook lean-to on the other side of the brook; it sleeps six, and water is available from the brook. From here, the trail rolls through fairly easy terrain to Golden Road (mile 99.3). Turn right and follow the road to Abol Bridge (mile 99.4), the terminus of this memorable trek.

There are numerous shelters along the Appalachian Trail, and it's legal to camp anywhere along the AT in the 100-Mile Wilderness; low-impact camping is encouraged.

User Groups: Hikers only. Dogs are discouraged along the Appalachian Trail in Maine. No bikes, horses, or wheelchair facilities. This trail should not be attempted in winter except by hikers prepared for severe winter weather; not suitable for skis.

Permits: A fee is charged for access to privately owned Golden Road; it has been $10 per vehicle in the past, but could change.

Maps: For a trail map, refer to maps 1, 2, and 3 in the *Map and Guide to the Appalachian Trail in Maine,* a set of seven maps and a guidebook for $25.00 from the Maine Appalachian Trail Club. For topographic area maps, request Rainbow Lake East, Rainbow Lake West, Wadleigh Mountain, Nahmakanta Stream, Pemadumcook Lake, Jo-Mary Mountain, Big Shanty Mountain, Silver Lake, Barren Mountain East, Barren Mountain West, Monson East, and Monson West from the USGS.

Directions: You need to shuttle two vehicles for this trip. From Millinocket, drive on Route 157 west through East Millinocket to Millinocket Road. Follow signs for Baxter State Park. About a mile before the park entrance, bear left onto Golden Road, a private logging road where you pass through a gate and pay a toll. Continue about seven miles to the private campground at Abol Bridge. Drive over the bridge and park in the dirt lot on the left, about 0.1 mile east of where the Appalachian Trail emerges at the road. Drive a second vehicle to Monson, and pick up Route 15 north for 3.5 miles to a large turnout on the right and the trailhead for the Appalachian Trail.

A fee-based shuttle to road crossings along the Appalachian Trail, as well as other hiker services, is offered by Shaw's Lodging in Monson, 207/997-3597, www.shawslodging.com. A hiker shuttle, free Kennebec River ferry service, and other hiker services along the Appalachian Trail in Maine are also provided by Rivers and Trails, 207/663-4441 or (in Maine only) 888/356-2863, www.riversandtrails.com.

GPS Coordinates: 45.3362 N, 69.5591 W

Contact: Maine Appalachian Trail Club, P.O. Box 283, Augusta, ME 04332-0283, www.matc.org.

22 HALF A 100-MILE WILDERNESS

47.8 or 51.6 mi one-way/4-6 days

🚶 4   △ 10

between Monson and Baxter State Park

BEST (

Backpackers seeking one of the most remote experiences possible in New England, but who don't have the time to hike the entire 100-Mile Wilderness—the stretch of the Appalachian Trail (AT) in northern Maine that crosses no paved or public road for 99.4 miles—can instead backpack "half a wilderness." The AT crosses the dirt Kokadjo-B Pond Road, identified on some maps as Johnson Pond Road, a logical place to begin or conclude a trek of either the northern or southern half of the 100-Mile Wilderness. The 51.6 trail miles from this logging road south to Route 15 are characterized by rugged hiking over a landscape dominated by low mountains boasting sporadic but long views of the forested landscape. The 47.8 miles of trail north to Golden Road at Abol Bridge have an entirely different personality, traversing mostly flat, low terrain around sprawling wilderness lakes. The southern portion can take five days or more; the northern is easier and can be done in four days by fit hikers. (See the trail notes in the *100-Mile Wilderness* listing in this chapter for a detailed description of both options.)

There are numerous shelters along the Appalachian Trail, and it's legal to camp anywhere along the AT in the 100-Mile Wilderness; low-impact camping is encouraged.

User Groups: Hikers only. No wheelchair facilities. Dogs are discouraged along the Appalachian Trail in Maine. Bikes and horses are prohibited. This trail should not be attempted in winter except by hikers prepared for severe winter weather; not suitable for skis.

Permits: A fee is charged for access to privately owned Golden Road; it has been $10 per vehicle in the past, but could change.

Maps: For a trail map, refer to maps 1, 2, and 3 in the *Map and Guide to the Appalachian Trail in Maine*, a set of seven maps and a guidebook for $25.00 from the Maine Appalachian Trail Club. For topographic area maps, request Rainbow Lake East, Rainbow Lake West, Wadleigh Mountain, Nahmakanta Stream, Pemadumcook Lake, Jo-Mary Mountain, Big Shanty Mountain, Silver Lake, Barren Mountain East, Barren Mountain West, Monson East, and Monson West from the USGS.

Directions: You need to shuttle two vehicles for this trip. To backpack the northern half of the 100-Mile Wilderness, from Millinocket take Route 157 west through East Millinocket to Millinocket Road. Follow signs for Baxter State Park. About a mile before the park entrance, bear left onto Golden Road, a private logging road where you pass through a gate and pay a toll. Continue about seven miles to the private campground at the Abol Bridge over the West Branch of the Penobscot River. Drive over the bridge and park in the dirt lot on the left, about 0.1 mile east of where the Appalachian Trail emerges at the road. Drive a second vehicle back to Millinocket. From the junction of Routes 11 and 157, go south on Route 11 for 15.5 miles and turn right (west) onto gravel Jo-Mary Road. Continue 0.2 mile and pass through a gate where a vehicle toll is collected. Proceed another six miles and bear left at a fork, following the sign for Gauntlet Falls/B-Pond (ignore the sign for the Appalachian Trail, which is also reached via the right fork). Continuing another 2.6 miles, bear right where the B-Pond Road branches left. At 14.6 miles from Route 11, the AT crosses the road 0.1 mile south of Crawford Pond; park off the road.

To backpack the southern half of the 100-Mile Wilderness, leave one car at the AT crossing of the logging road near Crawford Pond, then return to Route 11 and drive south to Monson. Pick up Route 15 north for 3.5 miles to a large turnout on the right and the trailhead for the Appalachian Trail at the 100-Mile Wilderness's southern end.

A fee-based shuttle to road crossings along the Appalachian Trail, as well as other hiker services, is offered by Shaw's Lodging in Monson, 207/997-3597, www.shawslodging.com. A hiker shuttle, free Kennebec River ferry service, and other hiker services along the Appalachian Trail in Maine are also provided by Steve Longley of Rivers and Trails, 207/663-4441 or (in Maine only) 888/356-2863, www.riversandtrails.com.

GPS Coordinates: 45.3362 N, 69.5591 W

Contact: Maine Appalachian Trail Club, P.O. Box 283, Augusta, ME 04332-0283, www.matc.org.

23 WHITE CAP MOUNTAIN
23 mi/2-3 days   🏃4 ⛺10

between Monson and Baxter State Park

At 3,654 feet, White Cap Mountain is the tallest peak in the 100-Mile Wilderness, the 99.4-mile stretch of the Appalachian Trail (AT) through northern Maine not crossed by paved or public roads. White Cap is also the last big peak in the Wilderness for northbound hikers and offers excellent views, especially toward Katahdin. A remote summit, White Cap can be reached on a two- or three-day trek via the logging road that accesses the AT.

From the logging road parking area, find the blue-blazed access trail on the north side of the pull-off and follow 0.2 mile to the white-blazed Appalachian Trail at the West Branch of the Pleasant River. You must ford this normally knee-deep channel of about 80 feet across to continue on (bring a pair of sandals or old sneakers for this stony crossing). The AT then continues over easy ground and among giant pines to the junction with the Gulf Hagas Trail, 1.3 miles from the river (see the *Gulf Hagas* listing in this chapter). The AT turns sharply right and ascends steadily northward for 4.2 miles, following Gulf Hagas Brook through dense forest to the Carl A. Newhall lean-to and tent sites, reached by a short side path off the AT; the lean-to sleeps six, and water is available from the brook.

Climbing steeply, the trail passes over the 2,683-foot summit of Gulf Hagas Mountain 6.6 miles from the road, where there are limited views to the west from just north of the true summit. After descending to the Sidney Tappen Campsite, the AT yo-yos north along the arduous ridge, over 3,178-foot West Peak (mile 8.2), with limited views, and the wooded summit of 3,244-foot Hay Mountain (mile 9.8). The trail dips again, passing a junction at 10.4 miles with the White Brook Trail (which descends east 1.9 miles to logging roads that eventually link with the road to Katahdin Iron Works). The AT then climbs to the White Cap summit. Enjoy impressive views towards Katahdin and return the way you came.

The Carl A. Newhall lean-to, with tent sites, is located 5.7 miles north on the AT from the parking area; and the Sidney Tappen Campsite, for tents only, lies 1.8 miles farther north. It's legal to camp anywhere along the AT in the 100-Mile Wilderness; low-impact camping is encouraged.

User Groups: Hikers only. No wheelchair facilities. Dogs are discouraged along the Appalachian Trail in Maine. Bikes and horses are prohibited. This trail should not be attempted in winter except by hikers experienced in mountaineering and prepared for severe winter weather; not suitable for skis.

Permits: No permits required.

Maps: For a trail map, refer to map 2 in the *Map and Guide to the Appalachian Trail in Maine,* a set of seven maps and a guidebook for $25.00 available from the Maine Appalachian Trail Club. For topographic area maps, request Hay Mountain, Big Shanty Mountain, Barren Mountain East, and Silver Lake from the USGS.

Directions: From Route 11, 5.5 miles north of Brownville Junction and 25.6 miles south of Millinocket, turn west onto a gravel road at a sign for Katahdin Iron Works. Follow it nearly seven miles to a gate where an entrance fee is collected. Beyond the gate, cross the bridge and turn right. Drive three miles, bear left at a fork, and then continue another 3.7 miles. As the road curves to the left, look for the parking area on the right (half a mile before the road's crossing of the Appalachian Trail).

This section of the Appalachian Trail is reached via a private logging road, and a nominal per-person toll is collected; children under 15 enter free. The access road isn't passable at certain times of year due to snow or muddy conditions.

GPS Coordinates: 45.4635 N, 69.2068 W

Contact: Maine Appalachian Trail Club, P.O. Box 283, Augusta, ME 04332-0283, www.matc.org.

24 GULF HAGAS
8 mi/5.5 hr 👫3 ⛺10

between Monson and Baxter State Park

BEST (

Known as Maine's Little Grand Canyon, Gulf Hagas is a deep, narrow canyon along the West Branch of the Pleasant River and not far from the 32-mile mark along the 100-Mile Wilderness. Taking in the sheer slate walls that drop for hundreds of feet into a boulder-choked, impassable river, it's easy to understand why the Abenaki gave it the name "hagas," their word for "evil place." The blue-blazed loop trail through the gulf is a 5.2-mile detour off the Appalachian Trail in the 100-Mile Wilderness, but the round-trip hike from the parking area is 8 miles. This trail goes through very little elevation gain or loss, but runs constantly up and down over rugged, rocky terrain; your hike could easily take more than the estimated 5.5 hours, especially when you start hanging out at the many waterfalls and clifftop viewpoints. Be forewarned: This is a very popular hike in summer, so expect crowds.

From the parking area, follow the blue-blazed access trail 0.2 mile to the white-blazed Appalachian Trail (AT) at the West Branch of the Pleasant River, a normally knee-deep channel about 80 feet across, which you must ford (bring a pair of sandals or old sneakers for this stony crossing to make it easier on the feet). Continue along the wide, flat AT and pass a side trail 0.2 mile from the river that leads to campsites at Hay Brook. At 0.3 mile, another side path leads about 200 feet into the Hermitage, a grove of ancient white pine trees, some as tall as 130 feet. The AT continues over easy ground among other giant pines to the junction with the Gulf Hagas Trail, 1.3 miles from the river. The AT turns sharply right, but continue straight onto the blue-blazed trail, immediately crossing Gulf Hagas Brook. Bear left onto the loop trail. At 0.1 mile, a side path leads left to beautiful Screw Auger Falls on Gulf Hagas Brook. At 0.2 mile, another side path leads to the bottom of Screw Auger. (The brook continues down through a series of cascades and pools, including some spots ideal for swimming.)

The Gulf Hagas Trail continues down to the canyon rim, weaving in and out of the forest to views from the canyon rim and dropping down to the riverbank in places. Significant features along the rim include Hammond Street Pitch, a view high above the river, reached on a short path at 0.7 mile; the Jaws Cascades (seen from side paths or views at 1.2, 1.4, and 1.5 miles); Buttermilk Falls at 1.8 miles; Stair Falls at 1.9 miles; Billings Falls at 2.7 miles; and a view down the gulf from its head at 2.9 miles. Three miles into the loop, turn right onto the Pleasant River Road, an old logging road that is at first a footpath but widens over the 2.2 miles back to the start of this loop. The logging road provides much easier walking and a faster return route than doubling back along the gulf rim.

User Groups: Hikers only. No wheelchair facilities. Dogs are discouraged along the Appalachian Trail in Maine. Bikes and horses are prohibited. Portions of this trail are difficult to ski or snowshoe.

Permits: No permits required.

Maps: For a trail map, refer to map 2 in the *Map and Guide to the Appalachian Trail in Maine,* a set of seven maps and a guidebook for $25.00 available from the Maine Appalachian Trail Club. For topographic area maps, request Barren Mountain East and Silver Lake from the USGS.

Directions: From Route 11, 5.5 miles north of Brownville Junction and 25.6 miles south of Millinocket, turn west onto a gravel road at a sign for Katahdin Iron Works. Follow it nearly seven miles to a gate where an entrance fee is collected. Beyond the gate, cross the bridge and turn right. Drive 3 miles, bear left at a fork, and then continue another 3.7 miles to a parking area (half a mile before the road crosses the Appalachian Trail).

Gulf Hagas is reached via a private logging road, and a nominal per-person toll is collected; children under 15 enter free. The access roads are not passable at certain times of year due to snow or muddy conditions.

GPS Coordinates: 45.4635 N, 69.2067 W

Contact: Maine Appalachian Trail Club, P.O. Box 283, Augusta, ME 04332-0283, www. matc.org.

25 BARREN MOUNTAIN AND SLUGUNDY GORGE

8 mi/6 hr 🥾4 ⛺10

northeast of Monson

By employing dirt logging roads to access this stretch of the Appalachian Trail (AT), you can make a one-day or an overnight hike into this picturesque and varied area of the 100-Mile Wilderness. What's here? The round-trip hike to the summit of Barren Mountain entails 8 demanding miles round-trip and 2,000 feet of climbing, but it's just 1.6 miles round-trip to picturesque Slugundy Gorge. Barren and Slugundy are reached by walking north on the AT. The one caveat about this hike is that Long Pond Stream can be very difficult to cross, so it's best to go in late summer or early fall, when water levels are down.

From the Bodfish Farm–Long Pond Tote Road, turn right (north) onto the AT. Within 0.1 mile, ford Long Pond Stream. The trail parallels pools and flumes in the stream for more than half a mile; after it turns uphill, a short side path leads left to Slugundy Gorge, a scenic gorge and falls. Just beyond, another side path leads left 150 yards to the Long Pond Stream lean-to. Behind the shelter, the AT begins the steep Barren Mountain climb. At two miles, a side path leads right about 250 feet to the top of the Barren Slide, from which there are excellent views south of Lake Onawa and Borestone Mountain. Following the ridge, the trail reaches the aptly named, 2,670-foot summit of Barren Mountain two miles beyond the slide, where there are sweeping views, particularly south and west; an abandoned fire tower stands at the summit. Continuing north on the AT for 0.9 mile brings you to a side trail leading right 0.3 mile to the beautiful tarn called Cloud Pond and the nearby lean-to, but to finish this hike, turn around and hike back the way you came.

The Long Pond Stream lean-to is along the Appalachian Trail 0.9 mile into this hike, and the Cloud Pond lean-to lies 1.2 miles beyond the summit of Barren Mountain. It's legal to camp anywhere along the AT in the 100-Mile Wilderness; low-impact camping is encouraged.

User Groups: Hikers only. No wheelchair facilities. Dogs are discouraged along the Appalachian Trail in Maine. Bikes and horses are prohibited. Portions of this trail are difficult to ski or snowshoe.

Permits: Parking and access are free.

Maps: For a trail map, refer to map 3 in the *Map and Guide to the Appalachian Trail in Maine,* a set of seven maps and a guidebook for $25.00 from the Maine Appalachian Trail Club. For topographic area maps, request Monson East, Barren Mountain West, and Barren Mountain East from the USGS.

Directions: From the center of Monson, drive half a mile north on Route 15 and turn right onto Elliottsville Road. Continue 7.8 miles to Big Wilson Stream, cross the bridge, and then turn left onto a dirt road. Drive another 2.8 miles to the Bodfish Farm, bear left at a fork and go 2.9 miles farther to where the white-blazed Appalachian Trail crosses the dirt road, known as the Bodfish Farm–Long Pond Tote Road; park at the roadside.

The dirt roads from Monson aren't passable at certain times of year due to snow or muddy conditions.

GPS Coordinates: 45.4168 N, 69.4203 W

Contact: Maine Appalachian Trail Club, P.O. Box 283, Augusta, ME 04332-0283, www.matc.org.

2 HOURS, 30 MIN

26 BORESTONE MOUNTAIN
4.5 mi/3.5 hr   🏃🏃3 ⛰9

in Borestone Mountain Audubon Sanctuary

Borestone Mountain (1,947 ft.) is a small, rugged peak located within a Maine Audubon Sanctuary just below the southern boundary of the 100-Mile Wilderness. Because the last timber harvest here was more than a century ago, the dense forest cover makes the mountain an attractive habitat for certain wildlife. Some of Maine's most coveted warblers spend their summer here—blackburnian and cape may nest in the coniferous canopy and goshawks wing through the mature deciduous woods to prey on grouse. Even pine martins are regularly seen by sanctuary staff. Expect lots of hikers with binoculars trained skyward while on this climb.

From the trailhead at the Bodfish Farm Road parking area, follow the gently ascending green-blazed Base Trail for 0.8 mile to the sanctuary's visitors center. Stop at the visitors center (9 A.M.–dusk daily, Memorial Day–October) to pay the entry fee for trail use. Here, you will also find nature displays, a gift shop, and restrooms.

Leaving the visitors center, the green-blazed Summit Trail crosses the outlet of Sunrise Pond (at the pond's southeastern end). Steadily ascending with good cover, you will notice the trail becoming rough and slippery about 1.1 miles out from the visitors center. Be prepared to scramble at the steepest sections. The trail keeps up a steady ascent and at 1.7 reach West Peak. Continue on for 0.25 mile down to a saddle and then climb a barren ledge to East Peak, the mountain's true summit. From here, look down on nearby Lake Onawa and across to 2,660-foot Barren Mountain. Return to the trailhead by the same route.

User groups: Hikers and leashed dogs only. No mountain bikes or horses. Sanctuary visitors center is fully accessible for wheelchairs (reach the center from a separate access road). This trail should not be attempted in winter.

Permits: Parking is free. Trail day pass fees are $4 adults and $3 students, children under 6 free (group rates available).

Maps: For a map of Borestone and the Boreston Mountain Audubon Sanctuary, contact Maine Audubon. For a topographic area map, request Barren Mountain East quad from the USGS.

Directions: From Monson, take Maine Routes 6 and 15 north 0.6 mile to Elliotsville Road. Turn right and continue on Elliotsville Road for 7.8 miles. After the bridge over Big Wilson Stream, turn left on Bodfish Farm Road and immediately cross the Canadian Pacific Railroad tracks. The trailhead is 0.1 mile past the railroad tracks and is well marked. Park across the road from the trailhead and make sure to leave your car out of the way of traffic.

GPS Coordinates: 45.3778 N, 69.4302 W

Contact: Maine Audubon, 20 Gilsland Farm Rd., Falmouth, ME 04105, 207/781-09, www.maineaudubon.org.

DOWN EAST

© PETER DAME

BEST HIKES

◖ Bird-Watching
Great Wass Island, **page 83.**

◖ Coastal or Island Hikes
Isle au Haut: Western Head Loop, **page 64.**
Dorr and Cadillac Mountains, **page 71.**
Great Head, **page 75.**
Ocean Path, **page 77.**

◖ Fall Foliage
The Bubbles/Eagle Lake Loop, **page 74.**

◖ Lakes and Swimming Holes
Jordan Pond Loop, **page 80.**

◖ Sunrises
Cadillac Mountain: South Ridge Trail, **page 81.**

◖ Sunsets
Isle au Haut: Eben's Head, **page 61.**

As Maine's jagged coastline stretches north and

east toward Canada, the bucolic landscape gives way to soaring granite cliffs and tall mountains so close to the roiling waters of the Atlantic, they seem to rear up from the sea itself. Here, too, are coastal meadows, salt marshes, cobblestone beaches, sky-high pine forests, and crystal-clear inland lakes. In New England and beyond — and whether you are an expert hiker, novice, or have kids in tow when you hit the trail — Down East harbors some of the best coastal hiking you'll find anywhere.

State parks dot the region and are excellent destinations for a day hike (especially Camden Hills State Park and Lubec's Quoddy Head), but Down East's centerpiece is Acadia National Park. Occupying 47,633 acres of granite-domed mountains, woodlands, lakes, ponds, and ocean shoreline, mostly on Mount Desert Island, Acadia is one of the country's smallest, yet most popular, national parks. Glaciers carved a unique landscape here of mountains rising as high as 1,500 feet virtually out of the ocean — most of them thrusting bare summits into the sky — and innumerable islands, bays, and coves that collaborate to create a hiking environment unlike any other. Designated with national park status in 1919, thanks in part to land donations from the area's wealthy summer residents (among them John D. Rockefeller), Acadia was the first national park established east of the Mississippi.

With more than 120 miles of hiking trails and 45 miles of gravel carriage roads, Acadia boasts almost endless possibilities for hiking, horseback riding, and mountain biking. Many of the park's most popular treks are relatively short in length, leading to spectacularly long views of mountains, ocean, and islands. And although some trails are steep and rugged, the majority of hikes in Acadia are suitable for younger children. All trails in Acadia are blue-blazed and cairns are frequent along rockier trails; trailheads are marked by signposts.

Isle au Haut (pronounced "eye la ho" locally), the outermost island in Penobscot Bay, serves as a remote outpost of Acadia National Park. Reached only by a small mail boat ferry from the mainland, the island is home to approximately 65 year-round residents who live on the edge of the parklands. Isle au Haut's many seasonal visitors have access to 18 miles of hiking trails on rocky coastline and low hills, with trailheads easily reached from the ferry landing at Duck Harbor.

Equal to the rugged beauty of the region's geography is Down East's eclectic mix of flora and fauna. Its cold, nutrient-rich seawater, high tidal ranges, and shoreline spruce forests create a unique boreal coastline – more similar to the fjords of northern Scandinavia than the sandy spits of southern New England. Thick with red spruce and white pine, Down East's forests are home to white-tail deer, red foxes, snowshoe hares, beavers, otters, and even the occasional moose; seabirds, hawks, peregrine falcons, and breeding warblers are just some of the many avian species spotted in the area. And a real treat for wildlife lovers: Look offshore almost anywhere along the coast and spot playful harbor seals sunning themselves at low tide. (Harbor seal populations are highest in spring and summer.)

July and August are crowded months on Mount Desert Island. May, June, September, and October are much less crowded; spring tends to be cool and sometimes rainy, while fall is drier, with its share of both warm and cool days. State parks in Maine don't see anywhere near the crowds of Acadia during the tourist season, making them a good alternative for those who want to enjoy Down East's scenic splendor in relative solitude. In winter, trails are almost empty of all but the hardiest of hikers as the weather turns brutally windy and cold, with frequent storms lashing the coast. Still, state parks and parts of Acadia do provide access year-round.

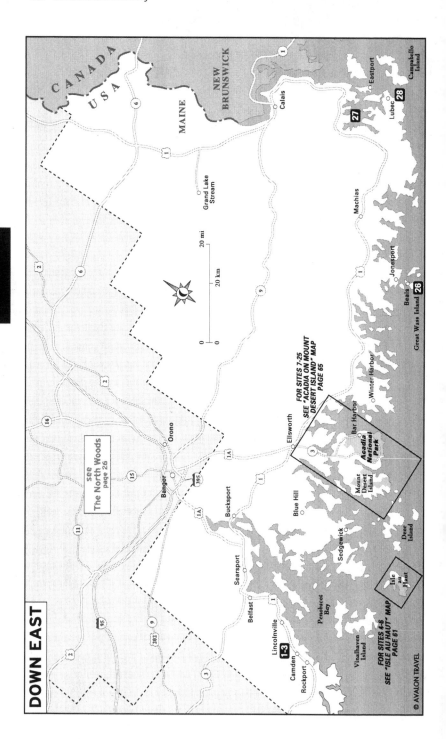

DOWN EAST

CANADA
USA
MAINE
NEW BRUNSWICK
Campobello Island
Eastport
Lubec
27
28

Calais
Machias
Grand Lake Stream
Jonesport
Beals
Great Wass Island 26

20 mi
20 km

0
0

FOR SITES 7-25
SEE "ACADIA ON MOUNT
DESERT ISLAND" MAP
PAGE 65

Bar Harbor
Winter Harbor
Acadia National Park
Mount Desert Island

Ellsworth

Orono
Bangor

see
The North Woods
page 26

Bucksport
Blue Hill
Sedgewick
Deer Island

Searsport

Belfast
Penobscot Bay
Isle au Haut

Lincolnville
Camden
Rockport

Vinalhaven Island

FOR SITES 4-6
SEE "ISLE AU HAUT" MAP
PAGE 61

1-3

© AVALON TRAVEL

1 MAIDEN CLIFF
2 mi/1.5 hr

in Camden Hills State Park

Tucked away along the northwest edge of Camden Hills State Park, the 800-foot Maiden Cliff soars high above sprawling Megunticook Lake and offers extensive views of the hills to the west. While it's a nice trek anytime, think about saving this hike for late in the day, when the sinking sun shoots sparkling rays across the lake and surrounding hills. For hikers who are new to Camden Hills State Park, a curious site on the cliff is the large wooden cross planted right at the cliff's edge. As a plaque near the cross explains, it commemorates the spot where a young girl named Elenora French fell to her death in 1864. According to local legend, she was attempting to catch her windblown hat when she fell over the almost sheer drop.

From the parking lot, follow the wide Maiden Cliff Trail, ascending steadily through the woods for a half mile. Bear right on the Ridge Trail, reaching an open area and the junction with the Scenic Trail in 0.3 mile. Turn left (northwest) on the Scenic Trail, following the cliff tops with outstanding views for nearly a quarter mile. The trail then dips back into the woods again to reach a junction with the Maiden Cliff Trail (marked by a sign) in another quarter mile. Continue ahead 100 feet to the cross and plaque. From here, double back and descend the Maiden Cliff Trail for nearly a mile to the parking lot.

User Groups: Hikers and leashed dogs. No bikes, horses, or wheelchair facilities.

Permits: Because the Maiden Cliff Trailhead is located outside the Camden Hills State Park perimeter, parking and access are free.

Maps: A basic trail system map, suitable for this hike, is available at the state park entrance on U.S. 1, two miles north of the Route 52 junction in Camden. For topographic area maps, request Camden and Lincolnville from the USGS.

Directions: From the junction of Route 52 and U.S. 1 in Camden, drive west on Route 52 for three miles to a parking area on the right (just before Megunticook Lake). The Maiden Cliff Trail begins at the back of the lot.
GPS Coordinates: 44.2822 N, 69.1018 W
Contact: Camden Hills State Park, 280 Belfast Rd., Camden, ME 04843, 207/236-3109 in season, 207/236-0849 off-season. Maine Department of Conservation, Bureau of Parks and Lands, 286 Water St., Key Bank Plaza, 3rd and 5th floors, Augusta, ME 04333-0022, 207/287-3821, www.maine.gov/doc/parks.

2 MOUNT MEGUNTICOOK TRAVERSE
4.75 mi one-way/3 hr

in Camden Hills State Park

Across the 5,500 acres of Camden Hills State Park, countless miles of hiking trails follow the coast and weave through the Megunticook Mountain range above the town of Camden, where the hills rise from near sea level to reach soaring heights. This fairly easy traverse of Mount Megunticook (1,380 ft.), the highest mountain in Camden Hills, combines good views from dramatic Maiden Cliff and scenic Ocean Lookout with a pleasant walk along Megunticook's mostly wooded ridge. A one-way traverse through the park, the hike climbs just over 1,000 feet.

From the parking area on Mount Battie Road, follow the Mount Megunticook Trail on a relentlessly uphill mile to Ocean Lookout. The trail's blue blazes start appearing at the hike's half-mile mark; stone stairs built into the hillside also start here to help with footing on the trail's steeper section. Reaching the lookout, take in terrific views south and east of the Camden area and even spot the famous windjammer ships cruising Penobscot Bay. Continue northwest on the Ridge Trail (look for the marker), passing over the wooded summit of Megunticook, a half mile beyond

Ocean Lookout. Continue over the summit on the Ridge Trail, and begin the relatively flat ridge walk. Approximately one mile past the summit, stay left on the Ridge Trail where Zeke's Trail branches right; then a half mile farther, stay right where the Jack Williams Trail enters from the left. Two miles past the summit, walk straight onto the Scenic Trail, following the open cliff tops with views of Megunticook Lake and the hills to the west. Dipping briefly into the woods again, in another 0.25 mile, you reach the Maiden Cliff Trail (marked by a sign). Before descending on the Maiden Trail, continue ahead 100 feet to Maiden Cliff; here a large wooden cross marks the spot where a young girl named Elenora French fell to her death in 1864. The cliffs seem to drop almost straight down into the lake. Double back and descend the Maiden Cliff Trail for nearly a mile to the parking lot on Route 52.

User Groups: Hikers and leashed dogs. No bikes, horses, or wheelchair facilities.

Permits: Parking and access are free at the Maiden Cliff Trailhead. To reach the Ocean Lookout/Mount Megunticook Trailhead, a fee of $3 per adult Maine resident/$4.50 per adult nonresident (age 12 and over) is charged at the state park entrance; senior citizens pay $1.50 and children under 12 years old enter free. The park season is May 15–October 15, although trailheads are accessible year-round. No staff is on duty and no fee is collected off-season.

Maps: A basic trail system map, suitable for this hike, is available at the state park entrance. For topographic area maps, request Camden and Lincolnville from the USGS.

Directions: Two vehicles must be shuttled at either end of this hike. From the junction of Route 52 and U.S. 1 in Camden, drive west on Route 52 for three miles to a parking area on the right (just before Megunticook Lake). The Maiden Cliff Trail begins at the back of the lot. Leave one vehicle there. Drive back to Camden and head north on U.S. 1 for two miles to the state park entrance on the left.

Past the entrance gate, turn left on Mount Battie Road and then right into a parking lot marked with a sign reading "Hikers Parking." The Mount Megunticook Trail begins at the back of the lot.

GPS Coordinates: 44.2311 N, 69.0470 W

Contact: Camden Hills State Park, 280 Belfast Rd., Camden, ME 04843, 207/236-3109 in season, 207/236-0849 off-season. Maine Department of Conservation, Bureau of Parks and Lands, 286 Water St., Key Bank Plaza, 3rd and 5th floors, Augusta, ME 04333-0022, 207/287-3821, www.maine.gov/doc/parks.

❸ OCEAN LOOKOUT
2 mi/1.5 hr

in Camden Hills State Park

Popular because of its wide views of the Camden area and the Penobscot Bay islands, this relatively easy hike leads to Ocean Lookout (1,300 ft.), a scenic open ridge on the otherwise wooded Mount Megunticook. Ocean Lookout makes for an enjoyable outing with adventurous kids or new hikers up for a challenge; the short, but relentlessly steady climb comes with a net elevation gain of almost a thousand feet.

From the parking area, pick up the Mount Megunticook Trail in the rear of the parking area at the trail marker. Initially an old woods road, in its first half mile, the trail enters a dense mixed forest, passes two trail junctions, and crosses a footbridge over a brisk stream. Blue blazes on the trees start to appear soon after the bridge crossing. Continue to follow the blazes as the trail steadily—and somewhat steeply—ascends to Ocean Lookout; stone steps at various spots along the trail make for easier footing. The wooded summit of 1,380-foot Mount Megunticook lies a half mile farther north on the Ridge Trail (see *Mount Megunticook Traverse* listing in this chapter), but this hike ends at the lookout. After you've taken in the bucolic beauty of Penobscot Bay, return the same way you came.

User Groups: Hikers and leashed dogs. No bikes, horses, or wheelchair facilities.

Permits: A fee of $3 per adult Maine resident/$4.50 per adult nonresident (age 12 and over) is charged at the state park entrance; senior citizens pay $1.50 and children under 12 years old enter free. The park season is May 15–October 15, although trailheads are accessible year-round. No staff is on duty and no fee is collected off-season.

Maps: A basic trail system map, suitable for this hike, is available at the state park entrance. For topographic area maps, request Camden and Lincolnville from the USGS.

Directions: The entrance to Camden Hills State Park is along U.S. 1, two miles north of the Route 52 junction in Camden. After passing through the entrance gate, turn left on Mount Battie Road and then right into a parking lot marked with a sign reading "Hikers Parking." The Mount Megunticook Trail begins at the back of the lot.

GPS Coordinates: 44.2311 N, 69.0470 W

Contact: Camden Hills State Park, 280 Belfast Rd., Camden, ME 04843, 207/236-3109 in season, 207/236-0849 off-season. Maine Department of Conservation, Bureau of Parks and Lands, 286 Water St., Key Bank Plaza, 3rd and 5th floors, Augusta, ME 04333-0022, 207/287-3821, www.maine.gov/doc/parks/index.html.

4 ISLE AU HAUT: EBEN'S HEAD
1 mi/0.75 hr

in Acadia National Park on Isle au Haut

BEST (

The Penobscot Bay outpost of Isle au Haut lies 15 miles southwest of Mount Desert Island. Home to a rural fishing village, complete with schoolhouse and post office, the island's six-mile long and two-mile wide expanse makes up a very remote section of Acadia National Park. Accessible only by a 45-minute mail boat

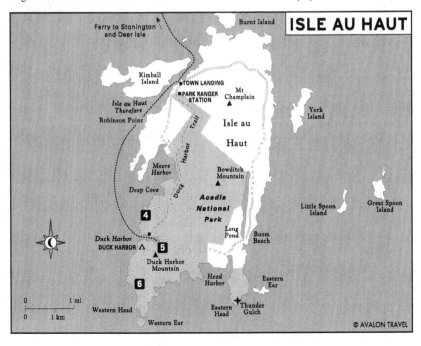

ISLE AU HAUT

© AVALON TRAVEL

VISITING ACADIA NATIONAL PARK AND ISLE AU HAUT

The park entrance fee to Acadia National Park is $20 per vehicle for a seven-day pass June 23–October 31, or $5 for walkers, bicyclists, or motorcyclists. The park entrance fee for vehicles is $10 May 1–June 22. A one-year vehicle pass costs $40. The Island Explorer shuttle bus provides free transportation from local lodges and campgrounds to points within the park and across Mount Desert Island late June–mid-October; contact Downeast Transportation, 207/667-5796, www.exploreacadia.com/index.html. Camping reservations can be made by calling 800/365-2267 or through the park's website. There are two campgrounds in Acadia: Blackwoods Campground, off Route 3 just south of Cadillac Mountain and east of Seal Harbor, is open year-round; Seawall Campground, off Route 102A east of Bass Harbor, opens in late June and closes after Labor Day.

Isle au Haut can be visited on a day trip or for overnight stays. A conveniently located campground near the ferry landing offers five lean-to shelters and a water pump. Lean-tos can be reserved May 15–October 15 by contacting the park; reservations are required. Reservations requests cannot be postmarked or made in person at park headquarters before April 1. Camping reservations cost $25 per site, regardless of the number of nights. Camping is limited to three nights mid-June–mid-September, and five nights the rest of the year. You can pitch a tent inside the lean-to only (which is advised in early summer, when the mosquitoes are vicious). Park rangers discourage bikes because of the limited roads, and bikes are prohibited from hiking trails. No wheelchair facilities are available.

ride from Stonington (no car ferry service is available), Isle au Haut rewards those who make the trip with plentiful trails, tall spruce forests, cobblestone beaches, and unobstructed ocean views. This hike leads to Eben's Head, a rocky bluff jutting into the ocean at the mouth of Duck Harbor, opposite the boat landing. For campers on the island, there is no nicer spot to watch the sunrise or sunset.

From the boat landing at Duck Harbor, turn left on the trail toward the water pump. Pass the trail branching right for the campground and continue straight onto Western Head Road. Follow it past the water pump and out to the main road. Turn left and follow the dirt main road around Duck Harbor. About 0.1 mile after the main road turns inland, you'll pass the Duck Harbor Trail on the right; then turn left onto the Eben's Head

Trail, which leads through woods out to that rocky bluff visible from the boat landing. Explore the rocky cove around Eben's Head, where interesting pools form at low tide. Return the way you came.

The Duck Harbor Campground has five lean-to shelters that can sleep up to six people each, and each lean-to site has a fire ring and picnic table. The lean-to shelters can be reserved May 15–October 15 by contacting the park (www.nps.gov/acad); reservations are required. Reservation requests cannot be postmarked or made in person at park headquarters before April 1. Camping reservations cost $25 per site, regardless of the number of nights.

User Groups: Hikers and dogs. Dogs must be leashed in the park and are prohibited in the campground. No bikes, horses, or wheelchair facilities.

Permits: No permits required.

Maps: A basic map of island trails and roads, suitable for this hike, is issued free to visitors arriving on the ferry or to those with camping reservations. The park website also has a map of Isle au Haut. Good trail maps of the area are the waterproof Acadia National Park (map 212) for $11.95 from Trails Illustrated (800/962-1643, www.natgeomaps.com/ti_212) and the Hiking and Biking Map to Acadia National Park and Mount Desert Island, $7.95 in waterproof Tyvek, from the Appalachian Mountain Club. For topographic island maps, request Isle au Haut West and Isle au Haut East from the USGS.

Directions: Isle au Haut is reached by mail boat/ferry from Stonington, Maine, to Duck Harbor, the starting point for the four Isle au Haut hikes described in this chapter. Round-trip cost is $35 for adults and $19 for children under age 12. The ferry is a small boat and does not transport motor vehicles (bikes are allowed).

To reach the dock where the ferry departs for Isle au Haut, take Route 15 to Main Street in Stonington and turn left at Bartlett's Market; the ferry landing is past the firehouse, at the end of the pier.

GPS Coordinates: 44.1578 N, 68.6643 W

Contact: Acadia National Park, P.O. Box 177, Eagle Lake Rd., Bar Harbor, ME 04609-0177, 207/288-3338, www.nps.gov/acad. Friends of Acadia, P.O. Box 45, 43 Cottage St., Bar Harbor, ME 04609, 207/288-3340 or 800/625-0321, www.friendsofacadia.org. Isle au Haut Boat Company, P.O. Box 709, Sea Breeze Ave., Stonington, ME 04651, 207/367-5193, www.isleauhaut.com.

5 ISLE AU HAUT: DUCK HARBOR MOUNTAIN/ MERCHANT POINT LOOP

4.5 mi/2.5 hr 🥾3 ⛰9

in Acadia National Park on Isle au Haut

Taking you out to rugged coastline, scenic coves, and jutting Merchant Point, this loop offers another way of hiking Duck Harbor Mountain. Try to time this hike for low tide when harbor seals are most likely to be seen lounging on off-shore rock outcroppings. Penobscot Bay is home to harbor and grey seals, as well as a few species of "ice seals" that occasionally wander south from subarctic regions. This hike traverses the mountain in the opposite direction from the Western Head Loop (see *Isle au Haut: Western Head Loop* listing in this chapter). It's easier going up the mountain from this side, so hikers squeamish about the rock scrambling on the Western Head side can hike up this way for the views, then just double back to Duck Harbor.

From the boat landing at Duck Harbor, turn left on the trail toward the water pump. Pass the trail branching right for the campground, and continue straight until you reach Western Head Road. Bearing left along the road, it's about 200 yards to the water pump (if you need water). For this hike, turn right on the grassy Western Head Road and follow it about a quarter mile, then turn left at the sign for the Duck Harbor Mountain Trail. Follow it a little more than a mile over several open ledges with commanding views of Isle au Haut's southern end. Reaching the trail's terminus at Squeaker Cove, turn left onto the Goat Trail, which moves in and out between woods and the coast. In less than a mile you reach a trail junction; left leads back to the dirt main road (where you would turn left for Duck Harbor), but bear right on a trail out to the rocky protrusion of Merchant Point (a great lunch spot). From Merchant Point, the trail turns back into the forest, crosses a marshy area, and reaches the main road. Turn left and follow the road a bit more than a mile to the head of Duck Harbor. Turn left onto Western Head Road, passing the water pump on the way back to the landing.

The Duck Harbor Campground has five lean-to shelters that can sleep up to six people each, and each lean-to site has a fire ring and picnic table. The lean-to shelters can be reserved May 15–October 15 by contacting the park (www.nps.gov/acad); reservations are required. Reservation requests cannot be postmarked or made in person at park head-quarters before April 1. Camping reservations cost $25 per site, regardless of the number of nights.

User Groups: Hikers and dogs. Dogs must be leashed in the park and are prohibited from the campground. No wheelchair facili-ties. The island rarely gets enough snow for winter activities. Bikes, horses, and hunting are prohibited.

Permits: No permits required.

Maps: A basic map of island trails and roads is issued free to visitors arriving on the ferry or to those with camping reservations. The park website also has a map of Isle au Haut. Good trail maps of the area are the waterproof Aca-dia National Park (map 212) for $11.95 from Trails Illustrated (800/962-1643, www.nat-geomaps.com/ti_212) and the Hiking and Biking Map to Acadia National Park and Mount Desert Island, $7.95 in waterproof Tyvek, from the Appalachian Mountain Club. For topographic island maps, request Isle au Haut West and Isle au Haut East from the USGS.

Directions: To reach the dock where the ferry departs for Isle au Haut, take Route 15 to Main Street in Stonington and turn left at Bartlett's Market; the ferry landing is past the firehouse, at the end of the pier. The round-trip cost is $35 for adults and $19 for children under age 12. The ferry is a small boat and does not transport motor vehicles (bikes are allowed).

GPS Coordinates: 44.1578 N, 68.6643 W

Contact: Acadia National Park, P.O. Box 177, Eagle Lake Rd., Bar Harbor, ME 04609-0177, 207/288-3338, www.nps.gov/acad. Friends of Acadia, P.O. Box 45, 43 Cottage St., Bar Har-bor, ME 04609, 207/288-3340 or 800/625-0321, www.friendsofacadia.org. Isle au Haut Boat Company, P.O. Box 709, Sea Breeze Ave., Stonington, ME 04651, 207/367-5193, www.isleauhaut.com.

6 ISLE AU HAUT: WESTERN HEAD LOOP

5 mi/3 hr

in Acadia National Park on Isle au Haut

BEST (

If you have time for just one hike on Isle au Haut, this is the one to take. It follows the stunning rocky coast around Western Head, offers the opportunity at low tide to wander onto the tiny island known as Western Ear, and climbs over 314-foot Duck Harbor Moun-tain, which boasts the best views on the island. Although much of the hike is relatively flat, the trail is fairly rugged in places.

From the boat landing at Duck Harbor, follow the trail leading left toward the water pump. Pass the trail branching right for the campground and continue straight until reach-ing Western Head Road. Bearing left along the road, it's about 200 yards to the water pump (if you need water). For this hike, take the grassy road to the right and follow it for less than a mile. Turn right onto the Western Head Trail, which reaches the coast within about a half mile. The trail turns left (south) and follows the rugged coast out to the point at Western Head, where that trail ends and the Cliff Trail begins. At low tide, you can walk across the narrow channel out to Western Ear. Be careful not to get trapped out there, or you'll have to wait hours for the tide to go out again.

The Cliff Trail heads northward into the woods, alternately following more rugged coastline and turning back into the forest to skirt steep cliffs. It reaches the end of Western Head Road in less than a mile. Turn left and follow the road about a quarter mile. When you see a cove on your right, turn right (watch for the trail sign, which is somewhat hidden) onto the Goat Trail. (The Western Head Road leads directly back to the Duck Harbor land-ing, a hike of less than two miles, and is a good option for hikers who want to avoid the steep rock scrambling on Duck Harbor Mountain.) Follow the Goat Trail along the coast for less than a half mile. At scenic Squeaker Cove,

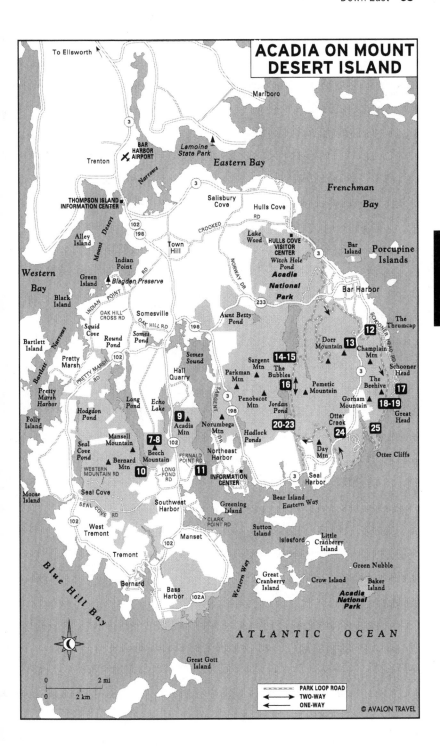

ACADIA ON MOUNT DESERT ISLAND

© LINDA MINER

lobster traps washed up on shore, Isle au Haut

turn left onto the Duck Harbor Mountain Trail; from here it's a bit more than a mile back to the Duck Harbor landing. The trail grows steep, involving somewhat exposed scrambling up rock slabs, and traverses several open ledges on Duck Harbor Mountain, with terrific long views of Isle au Haut Bay to the west (including Vinalhaven Island, the nearest piece of land across Isle au Haut Bay) and the Penobscot Bay islands and peninsulas to the north. The trail then descends to Western Head Road; turn right for Duck Harbor.

The Duck Harbor Campground has five lean-to shelters that can sleep up to six people each, and each lean-to site has a fire ring and picnic table. The lean-to shelters can be reserved May 15–October 15 by contacting the park (www.nps.gov/acad); reservations are required. Reservation requests cannot be postmarked or made in person at park headquarters before April 1. Camping reservations cost $25 per site, regardless of the number of nights.

User Groups: Hikers and dogs. Dogs must be leashed in the park and are prohibited from the campground. No bikes, horses, or wheelchair facilities.

Permits: No permits required.

Maps: A basic map of island trails and roads is issued free to visitors arriving on the ferry or to those with camping reservations. The park website also has a map of Isle au Haut. Good trail maps of the area are the waterproof Acadia National Park (map 212) for $11.95 from Trails Illustrated (800/962-1643, www.natgeomaps.com/ti_212) and the Hiking and Biking Map to Acadia National Park and Mount Desert Island, $7.95 in waterproof Tyvek, from the Appalachian Mountain Club. For topographic island maps, request Isle au Haut West and Isle au Haut East from the USGS.

Directions: To reach the dock where the ferry departs for Isle au Haut, take Route 15 to Main Street in Stonington and turn left at Bartlett's Market; the ferry landing is past the firehouse, at the end of the pier. The round-trip cost is $35 for adults and $19 for children under age 12. The ferry is a small boat and does not transport motor vehicles (bikes are allowed).

GPS Coordinates: 44.1578 N, 68.6643 W

Contact: Acadia National Park, P.O. Box 177, Eagle Lake Rd., Bar Harbor, ME 04609-0177, 207/288-3338, www.nps.gov/acad. Friends of Acadia, P.O. Box 45, 43 Cottage St., Bar Harbor, ME 04609, 207/288-3340 or 800/625-0321, www.friendsofacadia.org. Isle au Haut Boat Company, P.O. Box 709, Sea Breeze Ave., Stonington, ME 04651, 207/367-5193, www.isleauhaut.com.

🏃 BEECH MOUNTAIN

1.2 mi/1 hr   🏃2 ⛰9

in Acadia National Park

A bit off the beaten path, Beech Mountain (841 ft.), on Mount Desert Island's quieter western end, offers excellent long views without the crowded trail conditions that so frequently plague popular attractions on the east side of Acadia. Steep in sections, this loop hike takes you to open cliff ridges dropping to the shores of Long Pond and an abandoned fire tower summit; the route makes for an elevation gain of 832 feet. Best of all on Beech, if you long for a slice of solitude in this highly visited national park, you have a good chance of finding it here.

Pick up the Beech Mountain Trail where it leaves from a signpost in the parking area. Only steps into this hike the well-worn footpath reaches a fork. The loop can be hiked in either direction, but for best views, bear left. Heading steeply uphill through mixed birch and pine forest, you soon emerge onto an open ledge with terrific views east and north: from the islands south of Mount Desert to Acadia, Sargent, and Penobscot mountains and the myriad waterways to the north. A short distance farther up the trail is the summit, where trees block any view, but you can climb one flight of stairs on the closed fire tower for a 360-degree view. Beyond the summit, bear right onto the descent trail, which offers magnificent views over Long Pond and all the way to Camden Hills.

User Groups: Hikers and leashed dogs. No bikes, horses, or wheelchair facilities.

Permits: The park entrance fee is $20 per vehicle for a seven-day pass June 23–October 31, or $5 for walkers, bicyclists, or motorcyclists. The park entrance fee for vehicles is $10 May 1–June 22. A one-year vehicle pass costs $40. For U.S. citizens and residents over the age of 62, a lifetime Senior Pass is available for $10.

Maps: A basic park map is available at the visitors center and the park website (www.nps.gov/acad). Good trail maps of the area are the waterproof Acadia National Park (map 212) for $11.95 from Trails Illustrated (800/962-1643, www.natgeomaps.com/ti_212) and the Hiking and Biking Map to Acadia National Park and Mount Desert Island, $7.95 in waterproof Tyvek, from the Appalachian Mountain Club.

For a topographic area map, request Southwest Harbor from the USGS.

Directions: From the junction of Routes 198 and 102 in Somesville, drive south on Route 102 for 0.8 mile and turn right onto Pretty Marsh Road at the sign for Beech Mountain and the Beech Cliffs. Drive 0.2 mile, turn left onto Beech Hill Road, and then drive 3.1 miles to the parking lot at the end of the road. The trailhead is on the right as you enter. The park visitors center is located north of Bar Harbor at the junction of Route 3 and the start of the Park Loop Road.

GPS Coordinates: 44.3155 N, 68.3435 W

Contact: Acadia National Park, P.O. Box 177, Eagle Lake Rd., Bar Harbor, ME 04609-0177, 207/288-3338, www.nps.gov/acad. Friends of Acadia, P.O. Box 45, 43 Cottage St., Bar Harbor, ME 04609, 207/288-3340 or 800/625-0321, www.friendsofacadia.org.

8 BEECH AND CANADA CLIFFS
0.7 mi/0.75 hr 🏃1 ⛰8

in Acadia National Park

With very little effort required, the soaring cliffs above Echo Lake provide extraordinary views of Somes Sound and the St. Sauveur mountains to the east, the Gulf of Maine and the Cranberry Isles to the south, and Beech Mountain with its fire tower to the west.

From the parking lot, the almost flat Cliffs Trail quickly leads to the crest of land rising up from Echo Lake and to a trail junction. To the right is the trail to the Canada Cliffs, to the left the trail to the Beech Cliffs. Both entail a short walk of mere steps to some very worthwhile views. Explore both if you can, though Beech Cliffs may be closed in late spring and early summer to protect nesting peregrine falcons. The Canada Cliffs should be open all year. Once you've taken in the rugged majesty, retrace your steps back to the trail junction and parking area.

User Groups: Hikers and leashed dogs. No bikes, horses, or wheelchair facilities.

Permits: The park entrance fee is $20 per vehicle for a seven-day pass June 23–October 31, or $5 for walkers, bicyclists, or motorcyclists. The park entrance fee for vehicles is $10 May 1–June 22. A one-year vehicle pass costs $40. For U.S. citizens and residents over the age of 62, a lifetime Senior Pass is available for $10.

Maps: A basic park map is available at the visitors center and the park website (www.nps. gov/acad). Good trail maps of the area are the waterproof Acadia National Park (map 212) for $11.95 from Trails Illustrated (800/962-1643, www.natgeomaps.com/ti_212) and the Hiking and Biking Map to Acadia National Park and Mount Desert Island, $7.95 in waterproof Tyvek, from the Appalachian Mountain Club. For a topographic area map, request Southwest Harbor from the USGS.

Directions: From the junction of Routes 198 and 102 in Somesville, drive south on Route 102 for 0.8 mile and turn right onto Pretty Marsh Road at the sign for Beech Mountain and the Beech Cliffs. Continue 0.2 mile, turn left onto Beech Hill Road, and then drive 3.1 miles to the parking lot at the end of the road; the trailhead is on the left as you enter. The park visitors center is located north of Bar Harbor at the junction of Route 3 and the start of the Park Loop Road. GPS Coordinates: 44.3155 N, 68.3435 W

Contact: Acadia National Park, P.O. Box 177, Eagle Lake Rd., Bar Harbor, ME 04609-0177, 207/288-3338, www.nps.gov/acad. Friends of Acadia, P.O. Box 45, 43 Cottage St., Bar Harbor, ME 04609, 207/288-3340 or 800/625-0321, www.friendsofacadia.org.

⑨ ACADIA MOUNTAIN
2.5 mi/1.5 hr   🏃2 ⛰9

in Acadia National Park

Acadia Mountain (655 ft.) is the biggest hill on the west side of Somes Sound, the 168-foot

deep salt water gorge that nearly bisects the island—and the only true fjord in the eastern United States. From the park's namesake peak are excellent views of the sound, the towns of Northeast Harbor and Southwest Harbor, and the islands south of Mount Desert. Although it's a bit of a scramble on the way up, climbing about 500 feet, this easy hike is a good one for young children.

From the turnout, cross the highway to the trail. It soon forks; stay left, and in the next mile, cross a fire road (your route of descent) and proceed to the open, rocky ledges at the summit. The trail continues past the summit to even better views from ledges atop the mountain's east face. The trail then turns right, descending steep ledges with good views, and reaches a junction with the fire road (which resembles a trail here). Turn right, and the road soon widens. Just before reaching the highway, turn left onto the Acadia Mountain Trail, which leads back to the start.

User Groups: Hikers and leashed dogs. No bikes, horses, or wheelchair facilities.

Permits: The park entrance fee is $20 per vehicle for a seven-day pass June 23–October 31, or $5 for walkers, bicyclists, or motorcyclists. The park entrance fee for vehicles is $10 May 1–June 22. A one-year vehicle pass costs $40. For U.S. citizens and residents over the age of 62, a lifetime Senior Pass is available for $10.

Maps: A basic park map is available at the visitors center and the park website (www.nps. gov/acad). Good trail maps of the area are the waterproof Acadia National Park (map 212) for $11.95 from Trails Illustrated (800/962-1643, www.natgeomaps.com/ti_212) and the Hiking and Biking Map to Acadia National Park and Mount Desert Island, $7.95 in waterproof Tyvek, from the Appalachian Mountain Club. For a topographic area map, request Southwest Harbor from the USGS.

Directions: From the junction of Routes 198 and 102 in Somesville, drive south on Route 102 for 3.4 miles to a turnout on the right at the trailhead for Acadia Mountain (look for the sign marker). The park visitors center is located north of Bar Harbor at the junction of Route 3 and the start of the Park Loop Road.

GPS Coordinates: 44.3227 N, 68.3324 W

Contact: Acadia National Park, P.O. Box 177, Eagle Lake Rd., Bar Harbor, ME 04609-0177, 207/288-3338, www.nps.gov/acad. Friends of Acadia, P.O. Box 45, 43 Cottage St., Bar Harbor, ME 04609, 207/288-3340 or 800/625-0321, www.friendsofacadia.org.

10 BERNARD AND MANSELL MOUNTAINS
3.7 mi/2.5 hr

in Acadia National Park

While Bernard (1,071 ft.) and Mansell (949 ft.) are the two highest mountains on Mount Desert Island's west side, their summits are wooded, so these trails lack the spectacular views of other peaks in Acadia National Park. Still, this loop offers a scenic walk through the woods, is fairly challenging, lacks crowds of any kind, and does take you past a few good views of the bays and Long Pond. The cumulative elevation gain on this 3.7-mile hike is about 1,200 feet.

From the parking area, hike west on the Long Pond Trail, soon bearing left onto the Cold Brook Trail. In less than a half mile, cross Gilley Field and follow a road a short distance to the Sluiceway Trail on the right. It climbs fairly steeply to the South Face Trail, where you turn left for the Bernard Mountain summit, a few minutes' walk away. Backtrack and follow the trail down into Great Notch and straight ahead to the summit of Mansell Mountain. Continue over the summit, picking up the Perpendicular Trail, which descends the rugged east face of Mansell, often passing below low cliffs, to the Long Pond Trail. Turn right for the parking area.

User Groups: Hikers and leashed dogs. No bikes, horses, or wheelchair facilities.

Permits: The park entrance fee is $20 per vehicle for a seven-day pass June 23–October 31,

or $5 for walkers, bicyclists, or motorcyclists. The park entrance fee for vehicles is $10 May 1–June 22. A one-year vehicle pass costs $40. For U.S. citizens and residents over the age of 62, a lifetime Senior Pass is available for $10.

Maps: A basic park map is available at the visitors center and the park website (www.nps.gov/acad). Good trail maps of the area are the waterproof Acadia National Park (map 212) for $11.95 from Trails Illustrated (800/962-1643, www.natgeomaps.com/ti_212) and the Hiking and Biking Map to Acadia National Park and Mount Desert Island, $7.95 in waterproof Tyvek, from the Appalachian Mountain Club. For a topographic area map, request Southwest Harbor from the USGS.

Directions: From Route 102 in Southwest Harbor, turn west onto Seal Cove Road. Take a right onto Long Pond Road and follow it to the parking area at the south end of Long Pond (and a great view of the pond). The park visitors center is located north of Bar Harbor at the junction of Route 3 and the start of the Park Loop Road.

GPS Coordinates: 44.2991 N, 68.3493 W

Contact: Acadia National Park, P.O. Box 177, Eagle Lake Rd., Bar Harbor, ME 04609-0177, 207/288-3338, www.nps.gov/acad. Friends of Acadia, P.O. Box 45, 43 Cottage St., Bar Harbor, ME 04609, 207/288-3340 or 800/625-0321, www.friendsofacadia.org.

11 FLYING MOUNTAIN
0.6 mi/0.5 hr 🏃2 ⛰8

in Acadia National Park

Nearly bisecting Mount Desert Island, the glacially carved fjord, Somes Sound, is one of Acadia's most distinctive features. This short hike up Flying Mountain, a hill that rises just 284 feet above Somes (rhymes with homes), offers surprisingly nice views of the fjord from open ledges. The relatively small effort needed to reach this direct perch makes this a good hike for beginners and kids.

From the parking area, pick up the Flying Mountain Trail at the signpost. Ascending steadily from the start, the last stretch could seem a bit steep for some. Once on the ledges, be sure to continue to the true summit, marked by a signpost, where the views are often even better than those you see when you first reach the ledges. Retrace your steps to return to your car.

User Groups: Hikers and leashed dogs. No bikes, horses, or wheelchair facilities.

Permits: The park entrance fee is $20 per vehicle for a seven-day pass June 23–October 31, or $5 for walkers, bicyclists, or motorcyclists. The park entrance fee for vehicles is $10 May 1–June 22. A one-year vehicle pass costs $40. For U.S. citizens and residents over the age of 62, a lifetime Senior Pass is available for $10.

Maps: A basic park map is available at the visitors center and the park website (www.nps.gov/acad). Good trail maps of the area are the waterproof Acadia National Park (map 212) for $11.95 from Trails Illustrated (800/962-1643, www.natgeomaps.com/ti_212) and the Hiking and Biking Map to Acadia National Park and Mount Desert Island, $7.95 in waterproof Tyvek, from the Appalachian Mountain Club. For a topographic area map, request Southwest Harbor from the USGS.

Directions: From the junction of Routes 198 and 102 in Somesville, go south on Route 102 for 5.4 miles and turn left on Fernald Point Road. Drive one mile to a parking area on the left. The park visitors center is north of Bar Harbor, at the junction of Route 3 and Park Loop Road.

GPS Coordinates: 44.2994 N, 68.3162 W

Contact: Acadia National Park, P.O. Box 177, Eagle Lake Rd., Bar Harbor, ME 04609-0177, 207/288-3338, www.nps.gov/acad. Friends of Acadia, P.O. Box 45, 43 Cottage St., Bar Harbor, ME 04609, 207/288-3340 or 800/625-0321, www.friendsofacadia.org.

12 ACADIA TRAVERSE

13.5 mi one-way/10 hr

in Acadia National Park

Only have a day to spend at Acadia? If you are physically up for it, this traverse of Mount Desert Island's east side hits the park's six major peaks and spends much of the route above the trees, with sweeping views from a succession of long, open ridges. It's a long day: including time spent on short rest stops (but not including time spent shuttling vehicles), you may be out for 10 hours, finishing just before sunset. The cumulative elevation gain is about 4,700 feet—more than hiking up Mount Washington. And many of these trails—particularly the Beechcroft, the Cadillac Mountain West Face, and a section of the Penobscot Mountain Trail—are very steep. There are water sources on top of Cadillac Mountain and at the Jordan Pond House for refilling bottles.

Follow the Bear Brook Trail south to the summit of Champlain Mountain; within minutes of setting out, you enjoy views of the Frenchman Bay islands. Turn right (west) and descend the Beechcroft Trail 0.8 mile to the small pond called the Tarn (crossing Route 3). Ascend the steep Dorr Mountain East Face Trail, then turn right (north) onto the Dorr Mountain Trail and reach the open summit of Dorr (approximately one mile from the Tarn). Passing north over the summit, the trail becomes the North Ridge Trail and reaches a junction in 0.1 mile. Here, take a left for the Dorr Mountain Notch Trail. The trail dips 0.4 mile into the shallow but spectacular notch between Dorr and Cadillac Mountains and then climbs the open slope for half a mile to the Cadillac Mountain summit.

Descend the Cadillac Mountain South Ridge Trail for half a mile to the Cadillac Mountain West Face Trail, which drops very steeply for nearly a mile to a parking lot at the north end of Bubble Pond. Follow the carriage road south roughly 0.1 mile; then turn right onto the Pemetic Mountain Trail and take it over Pemetic's summit, 1.3 miles from Bubble Pond. Continue south over the long, rocky ridge for just over half a mile and then bear right onto the Pemetic West Cliff Trail. That trail descends 0.6 mile to the Pond Trail; turn right onto the Jordan Pond Trail, and descend easily another 0.4 mile to the Park Loop Road. Cross the road, enter the woods, and turn left on a trail to the Jordan Pond House. The Penobscot Mountain Trail begins behind the Jordan Pond House and leads 1.5 miles to the summit of Penobscot, at one point going straight up steep, rocky terrain. From the open summit of Penobscot, the Sargent Pond Trail heads northwest. Winding past Sargent Pond, the trail comes to a tiny alpine pond nestled among the conifers where it reaches a junction. Turn right (north) onto the Sargent Mountain South Ridge Trail, gradually climbing the long ridge to the 1,373-foot summit, a mile beyond Penobscot's, for the final panoramic view of this hike.

Descend west on the Grandgent Trail (be careful not to confuse it with the Sargent Mountain North Ridge Trail, which will add mileage to your hike at a time when you don't want it) for just over a mile to the top of little Parkman Mountain. (Note the trail signs before starting down off Sargent. Grandgent leaves from the summit heading due west. If you find yourself walking north, chances are you are on the North Ridge Trail.) Turn left onto the Parkman Mountain Trail, descending southward. You cross two carriage roads; at the second crossing, turn right and follow that carriage road a short distance to a connector leading left to the parking area on Route 198, a mile from the Parkman summit. Then take off your boots and vigorously massage your feet.

User Groups: Hikers and leashed dogs. No bikes, horses, or wheelchair facilities.

Permits: The park entrance fee is $20 per vehicle for a seven-day pass June 23–October 31, or $5 for walkers, bicyclists, or motorcyclists. The park entrance fee for vehicles is $10 May 1–June 22. A one-year vehicle pass costs $40. For U.S. citizens and residents over the age of 62, a lifetime Senior Pass is available for $10.

Maps: A basic park map is available at the visitors center and the park website (www.nps. gov/acad). Good trail maps of the area are the waterproof Acadia National Park (map 212) for $11.95 from Trails Illustrated (800/962-1643, www.natgeomaps.com/ti_212) and the Hiking and Biking Map to Acadia National Park and Mount Desert Island, $7.95 in waterproof Tyvek, from the Appalachian Mountain Club. For a topographic area map, request Seal Harbor from the USGS.

Directions: Two vehicles are needed for this traverse. Leave one vehicle at the northernmost of the two parking areas north of Upper Hadlock Pond along Route 198 in Northeast Harbor. Then drive to the hike's start, a turnout on the Park Loop Road at the Bear Brook Trail, 0.2 mile past a picnic area. If you're traveling with a group of friends, you might leave a third vehicle roughly halfway through the hike, at either the Bubble Pond or Jordan Pond parking areas, in case you can't finish the hike. The park visitors center is located north of Bar Harbor at the junction of Route 3 and the start of the Park Loop Road. GPS Coordinates: 44.3602 N, 68.1983 W

Contact: Acadia National Park, P.O. Box 177, Eagle Lake Rd., Bar Harbor, ME 04609-0177, 207/288-3338, www.nps.gov/acad. Friends of Acadia, P.O. Box 45, 43 Cottage St., Bar Harbor, ME 04609, 207/288-3340 or 800/625-0321, www.friendsofacadia.org.

🔢 DORR AND CADILLAC MOUNTAINS

3 mi/2 hr 🏃4 ⛰10

in Acadia National Park

BEST (

This moderate hike combines the highest peak on Mount Desert Island, 1,530-foot Cadillac Mountain, with its neighbor to the east, 1,270-foot Dorr, a mountain just as scenic but far less crowded. For much of this hike, you enjoy continuous views that take in Champlain Mountain, the islands of Frenchman Bay, and the rugged terrain atop Dorr and Cadillac. While just three miles long, this hike's cumulative elevation gain exceeds 1,500 feet.

From the parking area, turn left onto the Jessup Path and right onto the Dorr Mountain East Face Trail, which ascends numerous switchbacks up the steep flank of the mountain. Turn left onto the Dorr Mountain Trail; the trail actually passes just north of Dorr's true summit, which is reached by walking a nearly flat 0.1 mile south on the Dorr Mountain South Ridge Trail. Double back and turn left (west) onto the Dorr Mountain Notch Trail, which drops into the rugged—though not very deep—notch between Dorr and Cadillac. (This distinctive notch is visible from Route 3 south of the Tarn.) Follow the trail up the open east slope of Cadillac to the summit. Descend the way you came, but instead of turning right onto the Dorr Mountain East Face Trail, continue straight on the somewhat more forgiving Dorr Mountain Trail and then turn right onto the Jessup Path for the parking area.

User Groups: Hikers and leashed dogs. No bikes, horses, or wheelchair facilities.

Permits: The park entrance fee is $20 per vehicle for a seven-day pass June 23–October 31, or $5 for walkers, bicyclists, or motorcyclists. The park entrance fee for vehicles is $10 May 1–June 22. A one-year vehicle pass costs $40. For U.S. citizens and residents over the age of 62, a lifetime Senior Pass is available for $10.

Maps: A basic park map is available at the visitors center and the park website (www.nps.gov/acad). Good trail maps of the area are the waterproof Acadia National Park (map 212) for $11.95 from Trails Illustrated (800/962-1643, www.natgeomaps.com/ti_212) and the Hiking and Biking Map to Acadia National Park and Mount Desert Island, $7.95 in waterproof Tyvek, from the Appalachian Mountain Club. For a topographic area map, request Seal Harbor from the USGS.

Directions: Take Route 3 south from Bar Harbor or north from Blackwoods Campground, and turn into the parking area at the Tarn, just south of the Sieur de Monts entrance to the Park Loop Road. The park visitors center is located north of Bar Harbor, at the junction of Route 3 and the start of the Park Loop Road.

GPS Coordinates: 44.3556 N, 68.2048 W

Contact: Acadia National Park, P.O. Box 177, Eagle Lake Rd., Bar Harbor, ME 04609-0177, 207/288-3338, www.nps.gov/acad. Friends of Acadia, P.O. Box 45, 43 Cottage St., Bar Harbor, ME 04609, 207/288-3340 or 800/625-0321, www.friendsofacadia.org.

14 JORDAN POND/EAGLE LAKE/BUBBLE POND CARRIAGE ROAD LOOP

11.5 mi/6 hr   🥾5 ⛰️9

in Acadia National Park

This moderately hilly loop is one of the best carriage road trails in the park, passing high above Jordan Pond, circling Eagle Lake, and cruising along the western shore of Bubble Pond. Some may opt to bike this loop, but taking to the trail on foot gives you a better opportunity to savor every detail of this particularly lovely section of Acadia.

From the Bubble Pond parking area, follow the carriage road north along Eagle Lake. At the lake's northwest corner, turn left and follow the carriage road along the lake's western shore. After angling away from the lake (around Conners Nubble), turn right, then left, soon passing above Jordan Pond. At the pond's south end, turn left and cross the Park Loop Road. Follow this carriage road all the way back to Bubble Pond. Along the way, you pass a carriage road leading to the right across a bridge over the Loop Road; the loop beginning across the bridge climbs Day Mountain, a fun, if challenging, ride up and a fast ride down for mountain bikers who have the time and energy to add a few miles to this trail's distance.

User Groups: Hikers, bikers, leashed dogs,

skiers, and snowshoers. No wheelchair facilities. Horses and hunting are prohibited.

Permits: The park entrance fee is $20 per vehicle for a seven-day pass June 23–October 31, or $5 for walkers, bicyclists, or motorcyclists. The park entrance fee for vehicles is $10 May 1–June 22. A one-year vehicle pass costs $40. For U.S. citizens and residents over the age of 62, a lifetime Senior Pass is available for $10.

Maps: A basic park map is available at the visitors center and the park website (www.nps.gov/acad). Good trail maps of the area are the waterproof Acadia National Park (map 212) for $11.95 from Trails Illustrated (800/962-1643, www.natgeomaps.com/ti_212) and the Hiking and Biking Map to Acadia National Park and Mount Desert Island, $7.95 in waterproof Tyvek, from the Appalachian Mountain Club. For topographic area maps, request Seal Harbor and Southwest Harbor from the USGS.

Directions: Take Route 3 south from Bar Harbor to Seal Harbor. Turn right at the Acadia National Park entrance and left on the Park Loop Road, following it 2.6 miles past the Jordan Pond parking area to the Bubble Pond parking area. From the park visitors center, follow the Park Loop Road south. Where it splits, turn right for the Bubble Pond parking area. You can bike to the start from Blackwoods Campground, adding about seven miles round-trip: Bike Route 3 toward Seal Harbor and where the highway crosses a bridge over the Park Loop Road, carry your bike down a footpath to the Loop Road and follow it north. Just before the Jordan Pond House, turn right onto this carriage road loop. The park visitors center is north of Bar Harbor at the junction of Route 3 and Park Loop Road.

GPS Coordinates: 44.3354 N, 68.2510 W

Contact: Acadia National Park, P.O. Box 177, Eagle Lake Rd., Bar Harbor, ME 04609-0177, 207/288-3338, www.nps.gov/acad. Friends of Acadia, P.O. Box 45, 43 Cottage St., Bar Harbor, ME 04609, 207/288-3340 or 800/625-0321, www.friendsofacadia.org.

15 CADILLAC MOUNTAIN: WEST FACE TRAIL

2.8 mi/2.5 hr

in Acadia National Park

This trail offers the most direct and difficult route up Mount Desert Island's highest peak, 1,530-foot Cadillac Mountain. It involves a great deal of scrambling over steep slabs of open rock, relentlessly strenuous hiking, and about 1,200 feet of elevation gain. Descending may be more difficult than ascending. Much of the trail lies in the woods, but the occasional views—which become more frequent as you climb higher—down to Bubble Pond and of the deep cleft separating Cadillac and Pemetic Mountains are spectacular.

From the parking area, cross the carriage road and pick up the Cadillac Mountain West Face Trail at the north end of Bubble Pond. The trail rises sharply from the very beginning, following a rocky uphill path towards a large grove of cedar trees. Skirting left through the grove, the trail soon emerges onto the mountain's exposed face, a series of granite slabs broken only by patches of scrub vegetation. With so much rock, it's easy to lose the trail here; rely on the frequent trail cairns to help keep you on course. Wide-open, bird's eye views of the ocean and surrounding parkland may take your mind off the steep ascent. In just under a mile from the trailhead (and after a bit of a rock scramble at the very end), you top out on the mountain's South Ridge. Turn left onto the Cadillac Mountain South Ridge Trail and follow it to the summit. Head back along the same route.

User Groups: Hikers and leashed dogs. No bikes, horses, or wheelchair facilities.

Permits: The park entrance fee is $20 per vehicle for a seven-day pass June 23–October 31, or $5 for walkers, bicyclists, or motorcyclists. The park entrance fee for vehicles is $10 May 1–June 22. A one-year vehicle pass costs $40. For U.S. citizens and residents over the age of 62, a lifetime Senior Pass is available for $10.

looking toward The Bubbles from the southern end of Jordan Pond, Acadia National Park

Maps: A basic park map is available at the visitors center and the park website (www.nps.gov/acad). Good trail maps of the area are the waterproof Acadia National Park (map 212) for $11.95 from Trails Illustrated (800/962-1643, www.natgeomaps.com/ti_212) and the Hiking and Biking Map to Acadia National Park and Mount Desert Island, $7.95 in waterproof Tyvek, from the Appalachian Mountain Club. For topographic area maps, request Seal Harbor and Southwest Harbor from the USGS.

Directions: Take Route 3 south from Bar Harbor to Seal Harbor. Turn right at the Acadia National Park entrance and left on the Park Loop Road, following it 2.6 miles past the Jordan Pond parking area to the Bubble Pond parking area. Or from the park visitors center, follow the Park Loop Road south. Where it splits, turn right for the Bubble Pond parking area. The park visitors center is located north of Bar Harbor at the junction of Route 3 and Park Loop Road.

GPS Coordinates: 44.3354 N, 68.2510 W

Contact: Acadia National Park, P.O. Box 177, Eagle Lake Rd., Bar Harbor, ME 04609-0177, 207/288-3338, www.nps.gov/acad. Friends of Acadia, P.O. Box 45, 43 Cottage St., Bar Harbor, ME 04609, 207/288-3340 or 800/625-0321, www.friendsofacadia.org.

16 THE BUBBLES/EAGLE LAKE LOOP

4.2 mi/2 hr   🚶4 ⛰10

in Acadia National Park

BEST (

The Bubbles, the two 800-foot rounded peaks near the north shore of Jordan Pond really do look like twin pockets of air rising up from the pond's surface. This loop takes you to open ledges atop both North and South Bubble, with excellent views of Jordan Pond and the steep hills enclosing it. The loop also leads to Conners Nubble—a commanding overlook of Eagle Lake to the north of the Bubbles—and finishes with a walk along the rocky shore of Eagle Lake. A popular destination for summer tourists to Acadia, this loop may be at its best in September when the Bubbles glow with autumn color—an eye-popping treat for post-

Labor Day visitors to the park. For a shorter walk, the round-trip hike to the summit of North Bubble alone is 1.2 miles.

From the Bubble Rock parking area, the Bubble-Pemetic Trail heads west, then northwest through the woods, then turns sharply left, and climbs to the saddle between North and South Bubble within a half mile. Turn left to quickly reach the summit of South Bubble. Backtrack and ascend the North Bubble Trail to that summit, which is higher than the South Bubble summit. Continue over North Bubble, crossing a carriage road, to reach Conners Nubble in another mile. After taking in the view, descend and turn right onto the Eagle Lake Trail, dropping quickly to hug the lakeshore. At approximately 3.0 miles into this hike, turn right on the Jordan Pond Carry Trail and follow for about a mile back to the Bubble-Pemetic Trail, the return route to the parking area.

User Groups: Hikers and leashed dogs. No bikes, horses, or wheelchair facilities.

Permits: The park entrance fee is $20 per vehicle for a seven-day pass June 23–October 31, or $5 for walkers, bicyclists, or motorcyclists. The park entrance fee for vehicles is $10 May 1–June 22. A one-year vehicle pass costs $40. For U.S. citizens and residents over the age of 62, a lifetime Senior Pass is available for $10.

Maps: A basic park map is available at the visitors center and the park website (www.nps.gov/acad). Good trail maps of the area are the waterproof Acadia National Park (map 212) for $11.95 from Trails Illustrated (800/962-1643, www.natgeomaps.com/ti_212) and the Hiking and Biking Map to Acadia National Park and Mount Desert Island, $7.95 in waterproof Tyvek, from the Appalachian Mountain Club. For topographic area maps, request Seal Harbor and Southwest Harbor from the USGS.

Directions: Drive on Route 3 south from Bar Harbor to Seal Harbor. Turn right at the Acadia National Park entrance and left on the Park Loop Road, following it to the Bubble Rock parking area, 1.6 miles past the Jordan Pond parking area. Or from the park visitors center, follow the Park Loop Road south. Where it splits, turn right for the Bubble Rock parking area. The park visitors center is located north of Bar Harbor, at the junction of Route 3 and the start of the Park Loop Road.

GPS Coordinates: 44.3354 N, 68.2510 W

Contact: Acadia National Park, P.O. Box 177, Eagle Lake Road, Bar Harbor, ME 04609-0177, 207/288-3338, www.nps.gov/acad. Friends of Acadia, P.O. Box 45, 43 Cottage St., Bar Harbor, ME 04609, 207/288-3340 or 800/625-0321, www.friendsofacadia.org.

17 GREAT HEAD
1.6 mi/1 hr   🏃‍♀️1 ⛰9

In Acadia National Park

BEST (

This short, easy walk ascends 324 feet to the tops of tall cliffs rising virtually out of the ocean, offering spectacular views that stretch from the islands of Frenchman Bay to Otter Cliffs. It's a popular hike, but like many popular hikes, it tends to attract most folks during the day. Come here in the early morning or late afternoon for a less crowded visit. And this hike even gets a celebrity endorsement! Domestic mogul Martha Stewart, who owns a summer house nearby in Seal Harbor, calls Great Head her favorite hike in all of Acadia. When in the area, she often finds her way here to watch the sunrise.

From the parking area, follow the wide gravel path into the woods, soon reaching a trail entering from the left—the way this loop returns. Continue straight ahead, passing above Sand Beach (a trail leads down to the beach) and then ascending slightly. Where the trail forks, be sure to stay to the right, soon emerging at the cliffs. To return, follow the blue blazes north back to the gravel path and then turn right to head back to the parking area.

User Groups: Hikers and leashed dogs. No bikes, horses, or wheelchair facilities.

Permits: The park entrance fee is $20 per vehicle for a seven-day pass June 23–October 31, or $5 for walkers, bicyclists, or motorcyclists. The park entrance fee for vehicles is $10 May 1–June 22. A one-year vehicle pass costs $40. For U.S. citizens and residents over the age of 62, a lifetime Senior Pass is available for $10.

Maps: A basic park map is available at the visitors center and the park website (www.nps.gov/acad). Good trail maps of the area are the waterproof Acadia National Park (map 212) for $11.95 from Trails Illustrated (800/962-1643, www.natgeomaps.com/ti_212) and the Hiking and Biking Map to Acadia National Park and Mount Desert Island, $7.95 in waterproof Tyvek, from the Appalachian Mountain Club. For a topographic area map, request Seal Harbor from the USGS.

Directions: Drive on the Park Loop Road to the east side of Mount Desert Island, past the Precipice parking area. Immediately before the Loop Road entrance station (fee charged), turn left onto an unmarked road. Drive 0.2 mile, turn right, drive another 0.4 mile, and pull into a parking area on the left. The park visitors center is located north of Bar Harbor at the junction of Route 3 and the start of Park Loop Road.

GPS Coordinates: 44.3294 N, 68.1840 W

Contact: Acadia National Park, P.O. Box 177, Eagle Lake Rd., Bar Harbor, ME 04609-0177, 207/288-3338, www.nps.gov/acad. Friends of Acadia, P.O. Box 45, 43 Cottage St., Bar Harbor, ME 04609, 207/288-3340 or 800/625-0321, www.friendsofacadia.org.

18 THE BEEHIVE
1.3 mi/1.5 hr   👫4 ⛰10

in Acadia National Park

The climb up the cliffs on the Beehive's east face looks as if it's strictly for technical rock climbers when you stare up at it from the Sand Beach parking lot. The trail zigs and zags up ledges on the nearly vertical face, requiring hand-and-foot scrambling and the use of iron ladder rungs drilled into the rock. Though it's a fairly short climb, and just a half-mile walk some 400 feet uphill, this trail is not for anyone in poor physical condition or uncomfortable with exposure and heights. On the other hand, it's a wonderful trail for hikers looking for a little adventure. All the way up, you're treated to unimpeded views over Frenchman Bay and the coast, from Sand Beach and Great Head south to Otter Cliffs. On the summit, you look north to Champlain Mountain and northwest to Dorr and Cadillac Mountains.

From the parking area, cross the Loop Road and walk a few steps to the right to the Bowl Trail. You will soon turn onto the Beehive Trail and follow it to the summit. Continuing over the summit, turn left onto the Bowl Trail and make the easy descent back to the Loop Road. A very scenic and popular 3.7-mile loop links this with the Gorham Mountain Trail and Ocean Path (see *Gorham Mountain* and *Ocean Path* listings in this chapter).

User Groups: Hikers and leashed dogs. No bikes, horses, or wheelchair facilities.

Permits: The park entrance fee is $20 per vehicle for a seven-day pass June 23–October 31, or $5 for walkers, bicyclists, or motorcyclists. The park entrance fee for vehicles is $10 May 1–June 22. A one-year vehicle pass costs $40. For U.S. citizens and residents over the age of 62, a lifetime Senior Pass is available for $10.

Maps: A basic park map is available at the visitors center and the park website (www.nps.gov/acad). Good trail maps of the area are the waterproof Acadia National Park (map 212) for $11.95 from Trails Illustrated (800/962-1643, www.natgeomaps.com/ti_212) and the Hiking and Biking Map to Acadia National Park and Mount Desert Island, $7.95 in waterproof Tyvek, from the Appalachian Mountain Club. For a topographic area map, request Seal Harbor from the USGS.

Directions: Drive the Park Loop Road to the east side of Mount Desert Island and the large parking area at Sand Beach, half a mile south of the entrance station. The park visitors center is located north of Bar Harbor, at the junction of Route 3 and the start of the Park Loop Road.

GPS Coordinates: 44.3310 N, 68.1851 W

Contact: Acadia National Park, P.O. Box 177, Eagle Lake Rd., Bar Harbor, ME 04609-0177, 207/288-3338, www.nps.gov/acad. Friends of Acadia, P.O. Box 45, 43 Cottage St., Bar Harbor, ME 04609, 207/288-3340 or 800/625-0321, www.friendsofacadia.org.

19 OCEAN PATH
3.6 mi/2 hr   🏃2 ⛰10

in Acadia National Park

BEST (

This is one of the most popular hikes in the national park and for good reason. The Ocean Path follows the rugged shoreline from Sand Beach to Otter Point, passing over the top of Otter Cliffs—the island's tallest cliffs, popular with rock climbers. About midway along this trail is the famous Thunder Hole, where incoming waves crash into a channel-like pocket in the rocks, trapping air to create a loud and deep popping noise; it's most impressive around high tide.

From the parking area, the trail veers right. The shore here is mostly rocky, but constantly changes character over the course of this trail—some beaches are covered exclusively with small, round stones, others only with large rocks. As it approaches Otter Cliffs, the trail enters a small woods (across the road from another parking lot) and emerges atop Otter Cliffs. The trail continues beyond the cliffs to Otter Point, where it was extended a short distance in recent years to include a particularly scenic section right along the shore at Otter Point. Hike back along the same route.

Special Note: In the event of stormy weather or strong tidal surges, avoid this hike. In 2009, several people were dragged into the ocean near Otter Point by powerful waves,

the remnants of a passing hurricane. Always heed surf warnings issued by rangers and other park personnel.

User Groups: Hikers and leashed dogs. No bikes, horses, or wheelchairs.

Permits: The park entrance fee is $20 per vehicle for a seven-day pass June 23–October 31, or $5 for walkers, bicyclists, or motorcyclists. The park entrance fee for vehicles is $10 May 1–June 22. A one-year vehicle pass costs $40. For U.S. citizens and residents over the age of 62, a lifetime Senior Pass is available for $10.

Maps: A basic park map is available at the visitors center and the park website (www.nps.gov/acad). Good trail maps of the area are the waterproof Acadia National Park (map 212) for $11.95 from Trails Illustrated (800/962-1643, www.natgeomaps.com/ti_212) and the Hiking and Biking Map to Acadia National Park and Mount Desert Island, $7.95 in waterproof Tyvek, from the Appalachian Mountain Club. For a topographic area map, request Seal Harbor from the USGS.

Directions: Drive on the Park Loop Road to Mount Desert Island's east side and the large parking area at Sand Beach, half a mile south of the entrance station. The park visitors center is located north of Bar Harbor at the junction of Route 3 and the start of the Park Loop Road.

GPS Coordinates: 44.3310 N, 68.1851 W

Contact: Acadia National Park, P.O. Box 177, Eagle Lake Rd., Bar Harbor, ME 04609-0177, 207/288-3338, www.nps.gov/acad. Friends of Acadia, P.O. Box 45, 43 Cottage St., Bar Harbor, ME 04609, 207/288-3340 or 800/625-0321, www.friendsofacadia.org.

20 PENOBSCOT AND SARGENT MOUNTAINS
4.5 mi/3 hr   🏃5 ⛰10

in Acadia National Park

While nearly everyone who comes to Acadia National Park knows of Cadillac Mountain, few have heard of—and even fewer will actually hike—Penobscot and Sargent Mountains, which rise abruptly from the west shore of Jordan Pond. Yet the elevations of Sargent at 1,373 feet and Penobscot at 1,194 feet rank them as the second- and fifth-highest peaks on Mount Desert Island. And the ridge connecting them pushes nearly as much area above the trees as Cadillac's scenic South Ridge. For much of this 4.5-mile hike, which climbs more than 1,200 feet in elevation, you enjoy long views east to the Pemetic and Cadillac Mountains, south to the many offshore islands, and west across Somes Sound and Penobscot Bay to the Camden Hills.

From the parking area, head down the dirt access road toward Jordan Pond and turn left onto a trail leading about 50 yards to the Jordan Pond House. The Penobscot Mountain Trail begins behind the Jordan Pond House, soon ascending steep ledges that require some scrambling. After a rugged half mile, the trail reaches Penobscot's ridge, where the terrain flattens out somewhat and the hiking gets much easier. At 1.6 miles from the trailhead, the Penobscot summit is reached. Staying on the Penobscot Trail as it leaves the summit, in another 0.5 mile, dip into a small saddle between the mountains, soon reaching a trail junction. Here, turn left onto the Sargent Pond Trail, passing the small pond in the woods. Turn right onto the Sargent Mountain South Ridge Trail, ascending the long slope to the summit, marked by a pile of rocks. Just beyond the summit, turn right onto the Jordan Cliffs Trail, which traverses above the cliffs visible from Jordan Pond. Cross a carriage road and turn left onto the Penobscot Mountain Trail to return.

User Groups: Hikers and leashed dogs. No bikes, horses, or wheelchair facilities.

Permits: The park entrance fee is $20 per vehicle for a seven-day pass June 23–October 31, or $5 for walkers, bicyclists, or motorcyclists. The park entrance fee for vehicles is $10 May 1–June 22. A one-year vehicle pass costs $40. For U.S. citizens and residents over the age of 62, a lifetime Senior Pass is available for $10.

Maps: A basic park map is available at the visitors center and the park website (www.nps.gov/acad). Good trail maps of the area are the waterproof Acadia National Park (map 212) for $11.95 from Trails Illustrated (800/962-1643, www.natgeomaps.com/ti_212) and the Hiking and Biking Map to Acadia National Park and Mount Desert Island, $7.95 in waterproof Tyvek, from the Appalachian Mountain Club. For a topographic area map, request Southwest Harbor from the USGS.

Directions: Take Route 3 south from Bar Harbor to Seal Harbor. Turn right at the Acadia National Park entrance and left on the Park Loop Road, following it to the Jordan Pond parking area. Or from the park visitors center, follow the Park Loop Road south. Where it splits, turn right and continue to the Jordan Pond parking area. The park visitors center is located north of Bar Harbor, at the junction of Route 3 and the start of the Park Loop Road. GPS Coordinates: 44.3205 N, 68.2526 W

Contact: Acadia National Park, P.O. Box 177, Eagle Lake Rd., Bar Harbor, ME 04609-0177, 207/288-3338, www.nps.gov/acad. Friends of Acadia, P.O. Box 45, 43 Cottage St., Bar Harbor, ME 04609, 207/288-3340 or 800/625-0321, www.friendsofacadia.org.

21 JORDAN POND/SARGENT MOUNTAIN CARRIAGE ROAD LOOP

16 mi/8 hr

in Acadia National Park

Jordan Pond and the nearby lakes and wooded hills are popular destinations within Acadia, and this moderately hilly loop makes for a pleasant long-distance hike over several miles of broken-stone pathways. Part of the park's 45-mile carriage road system, the winding lanes were the brainchild of John D. Rockefeller as a way to encourage non-vehicular use of the park. This route could also make for an idyllic afternoon of biking or horseback riding,

© JAROSLAW TRAPSZO

Rosa rugosa (beach rose) flourishes along Acadia's carriage roads.

Pond—there's a view across the pond toward Sargent Mountain—and eventually contours around Sargent. Turn right at signpost 11 and in another 3.3 miles, pass almost straight through the intersection at signpost 13, heading south to pass Upper Hadlock Pond (on the right). At 1.5 miles past signpost 13, the carriage road makes a U-turn, passing by signpost 18. At signpost 19, take a right, travel a brief 0.9 mile, and then take a left at signpost 20. In another 1.2 miles, bear left at signpost 21 and in one more mile, take a right at signpost 14 to return to Jordan Pond. Pass signpost 15 to again reach signpost 16. Turn left at 16 to reach the Park Loop Road and the Jordan Pond Parking area.

User Groups: Hikers, bikers, leashed dogs, and horses. No wheelchair facilities. Hunting is prohibited.

Permits: The park entrance fee is $20 per vehicle for a seven-day pass June 23–October 31, or $5 for walkers, bicyclists, or motorcyclists. The park entrance fee for vehicles is $10 May 1–June 22. A one-year vehicle pass costs $40. For U.S. citizens and residents over the age of 62, a lifetime Senior Pass is available for $10.

Maps: A basic park map is available at the visitors center and the park website (www.nps.gov/acad). Good trail maps of the area are the waterproof Acadia National Park (map 212) for $11.95 from Trails Illustrated (800/962-1643, www.natgeomaps.com/ti_212) and the Hiking and Biking Map to Acadia National Park and Mount Desert Island, $7.95 in waterproof Tyvek, from the Appalachian Mountain Club. For a topographic area map, request Southwest Harbor from the USGS.

Directions: Take Route 3 south from Bar Harbor to Seal Harbor. Turn right at the Acadia National Park entrance and left on the Park Loop Road, following it to the Jordan Pond parking area. You can bike to the start from Blackwoods Campground, adding about seven miles round-trip: Bike Route 3 toward Seal Harbor, and where the highway crosses a bridge over the Park Loop Road, carry your

but for hikers, walking the carriage roads may be the best way to cover a wide swath of parkland without coming in contact with Acadia's often traffic-choked auto access roads.

For navigation ease, carriage road intersections within Acadia National Park are marked with numbered signposts. From the Jordan Pond parking area, go south on the Park Loop Road a short distance to a right turn onto the first carriage road you reach. Within a few feet, you will see a signpost marked 16. Here, take a right onto another carriage road and continue, passing intersections with carriage roads 15 and 14, and soon ascending a gradual slope above Jordan Pond. At approximately two miles into the hike, an intersection is reached at signpost 10. Turn right and in another 0.1 mile turn left at signpost 8 to follow the northwest shoreline of Eagle Lake. After 1.9 miles on this road, turn left at signpost 9.

Winding through the woods for 2.5 miles, the road passes secluded Aunt Betty bike down a footpath to the Loop Road; then follow it north and turn left onto a carriage path just before the Jordan Pond House. The park visitors center is located north of Bar Harbor at the junction of Route 3 and the start of the Park Loop Road.

GPS Coordinates: 44.3205 N, 68.2526 W

Contact: Acadia National Park, P.O. Box 177, Eagle Lake Rd., Bar Harbor, ME 04609-0177, 207/288-3338, www.nps.gov/acad. Friends of Acadia, P.O. Box 45, 43 Cottage St., Bar Harbor, ME 04609, 207/288-3340 or 800/625-0321, www.friendsofacadia.org.

22 JORDAN POND LOOP
3.3 mi/1.5 hr   👤2 ⛰8

in Acadia National Park

BEST (

In a park filled with so many glacier-carved lakes and ponds, Jordan Pond, on the western side of Park Loop Road, is perhaps the loveliest. This fairly flat trail loops around the scenic pond, allowing for constant gazing across the water to the steep mountainsides surrounding its peaceful waters—from the cliffs and rounded humps of the Bubbles to the wooded slopes of Penobscot and Pemetic Mountains. The easiest walking is along the pond's east shore; on the northeast and especially the northwest shores, the trail crosses areas of boulders that require some scrambling and rock-hopping. Although these patches are not too difficult to navigate, you can avoid them altogether by hiking in a counterclockwise direction and turning back upon reaching these sections.

From the Jordan Pond parking area, continue down the dirt road to the shore and turn right onto the wide gravel path of the Jordan Pond Shore Trail. At the pond's southwest corner, the trail reaches a carriage road; turn left over a bridge, then immediately left onto the trail again, soon reaching the famous view of the Bubbles from the pond's south end. Just beyond that, the trail completes the

loop at the dirt access road. Turn right for the parking lot.

User Groups: Hikers and leashed dogs. Bikes and horses allowed on carriage roads only. With assistance, some wheelchair users may be able to negotiate the east side of this hike. Contact the park for more information about accessibility at Acadia.

Permits: The park entrance fee is $20 per vehicle for a seven-day pass June 23–October 31, or $5 for walkers, bicyclists, or motorcyclists. The park entrance fee for vehicles is $10 May 1–June 22. A one-year vehicle pass costs $40. For U.S. citizens and residents over the age of 62, a lifetime Senior Pass is available for $10.

Maps: A basic park map is available at the visitors center and the park website (www.nps.gov/acad). Good trail maps of the area are the waterproof Acadia National Park (map 212) for $11.95 from Trails Illustrated (800/962-1643, www.natgeomaps.com/ti_212) and the Hiking and Biking Map to Acadia National Park and Mount Desert Island, $7.95 in waterproof Tyvek, from the Appalachian Mountain Club. For topographic area maps, request Seal Harbor and Southwest Harbor from the USGS.

Directions: Take Route 3 south from Bar Harbor to Seal Harbor. Turn right at the Acadia National Park entrance and left on the Park Loop Road, following it to the Jordan Pond parking area. Or from the park visitors center, follow the Park Loop Road south. Where it splits, turn right for the Jordan Pond parking area. The park visitors center is located north of Bar Harbor at the junction of Route 3 and the start of the Park Loop Road.

GPS Coordinates: 44.3205 N, 68.2526 W

Contact: Acadia National Park, P.O. Box 177, Eagle Lake Rd., Bar Harbor, ME 04609-0177, 207/288-3338, www.nps.gov/acad. Friends of Acadia, P.O. Box 45, 43 Cottage St., Bar Harbor, ME 04609, 207/288-3340 or 800/625-0321, www.friendsofacadia.org.

ꆷ PEMETIC MOUNTAIN

3.3 mi/2.5 hr   🏃3 ⛰10

in Acadia National Park

Pemetic Mountain, situated between Jordan Pond to the west and Bubble Pond and Cadillac Mountain to the east, thrusts a long, open ridge of rock into the sky. Its summit, at 1,284 feet, offers sweeping views—but it's the walk along the ridge that makes this hike memorable. The views take in Cadillac, Penobscot, and Sargent Mountains, the islands south of Mount Desert, and Jordan Pond, and offer a unique perspective on the Bubbles. The elevation gain is just under 1,000 feet.

From the Jordan Pond parking area, follow the dirt access road to the southeast shore of Jordan Pond. Turn left, follow the Jordan Pond Shore Trail a short distance, and then turn left onto the Pond Trail. Cross the Park Loop Road and in less than a half mile, turn left onto the Pemetic Mountain West Cliff Trail, ascending the ridge. At the junction with the Pemetic Mountain Trail, turn left (north) and proceed to the summit. Double back and follow the Pemetic Mountain Trail all the way to the Pond Trail, then turn right to go back the way you came.

User Groups: Hikers and leashed dogs. No bikes, horses, or wheelchair facilities.

Permits: The park entrance fee is $20 per vehicle for a seven-day pass June 23–October 31, or $5 for walkers, bicyclists, or motorcyclists. The park entrance fee for vehicles is $10 May 1–June 22. A one-year vehicle pass costs $40. For U.S. citizens and residents over the age of 62, a lifetime Senior Pass is available for $10.

Maps: A basic park map is available at the visitors center and the park website (www.nps.gov/acad). Good trail maps of the area are the waterproof Acadia National Park (map 212) for $11.95 from Trails Illustrated (800/962-1643, www.natgeomaps.com/ti_212) and the Hiking and Biking Map to Acadia National Park and Mount Desert Island, $7.95

in waterproof Tyvek, from the Appalachian Mountain Club. For topographic area maps, request Seal Harbor and Southwest Harbor from the USGS.

Directions: Take Route 3 south from Bar Harbor to Seal Harbor. Turn right at the Acadia National Park entrance and left on the Park Loop Road, following it to the Jordan Pond parking area. Or from the park visitors center, follow the Park Loop Road south. Where it splits, turn right and continue to the Jordan Pond parking area. The park visitors center is located north of Bar Harbor at the junction of Route 3 and the start of the Park Loop Road.

GPS Coordinates: 44.3205 N, 68.2526 W

Contact: Acadia National Park, P.O. Box 177, Eagle Lake Rd., Bar Harbor, ME 04609-0177, 207/288-3338, www.nps.gov/acad. Friends of Acadia, P.O. Box 45, 43 Cottage St., Bar Harbor, ME 04609, 207/288-3340 or 800/625-0321, www.friendsofacadia.org.

ꆸ CADILLAC MOUNTAIN: SOUTH RIDGE TRAIL

7 mi/4 hr   🏃5 ⛰10

in Acadia National Park

BEST (

The long, spectacular, wide-open South Ridge on the highest peak on Mount Desert Island—1,530-foot Cadillac Mountain—affords one of the longest and most scenic hikes in Acadia National Park. How many mountain ridges offer views not only of surrounding hills, but also of the ocean and a profusion of islands? A relatively short and somewhat steep hike through the woods brings you onto the broad ridge; then you have a long, uphill walk accompanied by sweeping views all the way to the summit. This seven-mile round-tripper climbs about 1,300 feet, making it one of the most challenging outings in the park. For campers staying at nearby Blackwoods Campground, make the easy mile-long climb to Eagles Crag (702 ft.) in the moments just before dawn and come prepared for an unbelievable sunrise. As the highest point on the North Atlantic seaboard, Cadillac Mountain is one of the first places in the United States to greet the rising sun.

From the roadside parking area, pickup the Cadillac Mountain South Ridge Trail as it enters the woods about 50 yards past the campground entrance road on the right (look for the trail marker). Starting off as a pleasant uphill walk through the woods, at 1.0 mile from Route 3, take the loop trail out to Eagles Crag (702 ft.), which offers views to the east; the loop trail rejoins the South Ridge Trail in 0.2 mile. Continuing up the South Ridge Trail, by 1.5 miles, the trail breaks out above the trees to views west to Pemetic and Sargent Mountains, and east and south to Frenchman Bay and numerous islands. At three miles, the trail passes a junction with the Cadillac Mountain West Face Trail (which descends left, or west), reaches a switchback in the paved summit road, and veers right, winding another half mile to the summit. Return the same way you came.

User Groups: Hikers and leashed dogs. No bikes, horses, or wheelchair facilities.

Permits: The park entrance fee is $20 per vehicle for a seven-day pass June 23–October 31, or $5 for walkers, bicyclists, or motorcyclists. The park entrance fee for vehicles is $10 May 1–June 22. A one-year vehicle pass costs $40. For U.S. citizens and residents over the age of 62, a lifetime Senior Pass is available for $10.

Maps: A basic park map is available at the visitors center and the park website (www.nps.gov/acad). Good trail maps of the area are the waterproof Acadia National Park (map 212) for $11.95 from Trails Illustrated (800/962-1643, www.natgeomaps.com/ti_212) and the Hiking and Biking Map to Acadia National Park and Mount Desert Island, $7.95 in waterproof Tyvek, from the Appalachian Mountain Club. For a topographic area map, request Seal Harbor from the USGS.

Directions: Take Route 3 south from Bar Harbor to the Blackwoods Campground entrance. The Cadillac Mountain South Ridge Trail enters the woods on the right about 50 yards past the campground entrance road; there is parking at the roadside. Campers in Blackwoods can pick up the trail at the west end of the campground's south loop (adding 1.4 miles to the hike's round-trip distance). The park visitors center is located north of Bar Harbor, at the junction of Route 3 and the start of the Park Loop Road.

GPS Coordinates: 44.3132 N, 68.2144 W

Contact: Acadia National Park, P.O. Box 177, Eagle Lake Rd., Bar Harbor, ME 04609-0177, 207/288-3338, www.nps.gov/acad. Friends of Acadia, P.O. Box 45, 43 Cottage St., Bar Harbor, ME 04609, 207/288-3340 or 800/625-0321, www.friendsofacadia.org.

25 GORHAM MOUNTAIN
2 mi/1.5 hr   🚶2 ⛰10

in Acadia National Park

On the southeastern edge of Mount Desert Island, this spectacular and all-too-brief climb along the open ridge of Gorham Mountain leads to continuous views of Acadia's coast and countless islands spun out across the bay. At 525 feet in elevation, Gorham is but a tiny hill compared to some of the park's loftier peaks. But because of Gorham's coastal location, the close views of the roiling sea are intimate and truly powerful. Reaching the rocky crown in just a mile, the trail grows rugged in spots as it nears the Cadillac Cliffs.

From the parking area, follow the Gorham Mountain Trail, at first an easy steady climb through a spruce forest. As the trees give way to a gradually steepening granite ascent, the trail reaches a split. Bear left to continue on the Gorham Mountain Trail. Or, for a more rugged route, bear right to follow the Cadillac Cliffs Trail, passing below the cliffs with rocky outcroppings overhead in places and loose rock underfoot. Some love this kind of trail adventure; others abhor it. Whichever path you take, the two trails rejoin just below the summit. Drink in the views from the top and then retrace your steps. (For better footing, even adventurers should consider descending the Gorham Mountain Trail all the way down.)

User Groups: Hikers and leashed dogs. No bikes, horses, or wheelchair facilities.

Permits: The park entrance fee is $20 per vehicle for a seven-day pass June 23–October 31, or $5 for walkers, bicyclists, or motorcyclists. The park entrance fee for vehicles is $10 May 1–June 22. A one-year vehicle pass costs $40. For U.S. citizens and residents over the age of 62, a lifetime Senior Pass is available for $10.

Maps: A basic park map is available at the visitors center and the park website (www.nps. gov/acad). Good trail maps of the area are the waterproof Acadia National Park (map 212) for $11.95 from Trails Illustrated (800/962-1643, www.natgeomaps.com/ti_212) and the Hiking and Biking Map to Acadia National Park and Mount Desert Island, $7.95 in waterproof Tyvek, from the Appalachian Mountain Club. For a topographic area map, request Seal Harbor from the USGS.

Directions: Take the Park Loop Road to the east side of Mount Desert Island and the parking area at the Gorham Mountain Trail and Monument Cove, south of Sand Beach and north of Otter Cliffs. The park visitors center is located north of Bar Harbor at the junction of Route 3 and the start of the Park Loop Road.

GPS Coordinates: 44.3167 N, 68.1913 W

Contact: Acadia National Park, P.O. Box 177, Eagle Lake Rd., Bar Harbor, ME 04609-0177, 207/288-3338, www.nps.gov/acad. Friends of Acadia, P.O. Box 45, 43 Cottage St., Bar Harbor, ME 04609, 207/288-3340 or 800/625-0321, www.friendsofacadia.org.

🗒26 GREAT WASS ISLAND
5 mi/2.5 hr   👫2 ⛰8

In Jonesport

BEST (

Connected to mainland Jonesport by bridge, Great Wass Island, covering six square miles, is the biggest island in the Great Wass Archipelago, a chain of over 43 hunks of rock extending far off the Down East coast. Much of Great Wass is a Nature Conservancy preserve, open to the public for hiking and bird-watching. The island's windswept, North Atlantic terrain, kept cold by the currents of the nearby Bay of Fundy, makes it a popular nesting grounds for virtually all boreal (subartic) birds in the state of Maine, including palm warblers, boreal chickadees, spruce grouse, yellow-bellied flycatchers, and black beak woodpeckers. Nesting takes place continuously during the warmer summer months. You can also see large numbers of harbor seals lounging at low tide just offshore. And on clear days, look far offshore for a glimpse of the distant Moose Peak lighthouse, built in 1851 on a remote island to the east (and still in operation). This loop of about five miles takes you deep into the island's boreal forest of jack pine and spruce and out to open, rocky ledges for breathtaking views.

From the parking area, leave on the unmarked trail (a well-worn path). In approximately 100 yards, the trail reaches a fork. Bear right on the Little Cove Trail; the Mud Hole Trail to the left is the one you will return on. For the next two miles, wander along the Little Cove Trail as it passes through a lush boreal forest of cold-loving conifers. Carpeting the forest floor is a velvety, electric green moss that springs underfoot. It's beautiful, but when wet, the moss can be very slippery. Breaks in tree cover give way along the trail in various places to open ledges of the island's best bog areas. Reaching the crashing shoreline, a red marker and cairn indicate the end of the trail. Turn left and follow the shore about a half-mile to another cairn and red marker at Mud Hole Point. The Mud Hole Trail follows a narrow cove for its first half-mile and is a good place for birding and seal watching. Reentering the boreal forest, the hike continues as a pleasant woods walk until reaching the junction with the Little Cove Trail. Turn right to return 100 yards back to the parking area.

Special Note: The rocky stretch of shore connecting the two trails may be tricky for some, especially at hide tide when the rocks will most likely be wet. If necessary, turn back and return to your car on the Little Cove Trail.

User Groups: Hikers and leashed dogs. No bikes, horses, or wheelchair facilities.

Permits: Parking and access are free.

Maps: A free trail map is available at the trailhead. For a topographic area map, request Great Wass Island from the USGS.

Directions: Cross the bridge from Jonesport to Beals Island (across from Tall Barney's Restaurant). Turn left at the end of the bridge, continue through one stop sign and cross a short causeway to Great Wass Island; make the first right immediately after the causeway and continue for 2.6 miles on a road that turns to gravel. Look for the Nature Conservancy parking lot on the left.

GPS Coordinates: 44.5060 N, 67.6004 W

Contact: The Nature Conservancy of Maine, 4 Maine St., Brunswick, ME 04011, 207/729-5181.

27 COBSCOOK BAY STATE PARK
1.8 mi/1 hr   👣1 ⛰8

in Edmunds Township

The Cobscook Bay estuary is a narrow opening to the sea that simply teems with wildlife. Eagles, ospreys, seals, otters, and even the occasional bear enjoy the bay's abundant fish populations, including smelt, alewives, shad, sea-run brook trout, striped bass and Atlantic salmon. Also found here are shellfish, marine worms, and other estuarine creatures. The park itself is an 888-acre peninsula thrust out into the bay, with trails providing good opportunities to observe the ebb and flow of the region's impressive tides. Cobscook, the Maliseet-Passamaquoddy tribal word for "boiling tides," aptly describes this setting where the tidal range averages 24 feet and can reach 28 feet (compared to a 9-foot average tide along Maine's southernmost coast). This trail leads to one of the park's largest coves and is an excellent place for nature observation and bird-watching.

From the parking area near the campground, pick up the Nature Trail, marked with a sign. Follow the trail an easy 0.6 mile to reach the shore of Cobscook's Burnt Cove. Come here in fall and at low tide, large groups of shorebirds can be seen along the mudflats and eel grass, a rest and refueling stop during seasonal migrations. Burnt Cove and other coves in the bay support a quarter of Maine's wintering black ducks and the state's highest concentration of bald eagles. (Be sure to ask for the free birding list for Cobscook Bay available at the park entrance.) Continue on the Nature Trail for another 0.3 mile to where it ends at the campground. Retrace your steps back to the parking area. Before you leave, cross the park access road and make a quick 0.4 mile round-trip to the park's fire tower lookout for long views of the bay.

User Groups: Hikers and leashed dogs. No bikes, horses, or wheelchair facilities.

Permits: A fee of $3 per adult Maine resident or $4.50 per adult nonresident (age 12 and over) is charged at the state park entrance; senior citizens pay $1.50 and children under 12 years old enter free. The park season is May 15–October 15, although trailheads are accessible year-round. No staff is on duty and no fee is collected off-season.

Maps: A free trail map, suitable for this hike, is available at the state park entrance. For a topographic map of trails, request Eastport from the USGS.

Directions: Take U.S. 1 to Edmunds and look for park signs marking the turnoff onto South Edmunds Road. The main park entrance is on the right 0.5 mile from the turnoff.

GPS Coordinates: 44.8505 N, 67.1544 W

Contact: Cobscook Bay State Park, 40 South Edmunds Rd., Edmunds Township, ME 04628, 207/726-4412, www.maine.gov/doc/parks/index.html.

28 QUODDY HEAD STATE PARK

3.6 mi/2 hr   👥2 ⛰9

in Lubec

Quoddy Head State Park is a rugged, 541-acre stretch of coast at the tip of America's easternmost peninsula, capped by the West Quoddy Head Light, the easternmost lighthouse in the United States. Trails through the park lead to some of Maine's best wildlife-watching areas. In summer, you may spot humpback, minke, and finback whales offshore, along with rafts of eider, scoter, and old squaw ducks. This loop hike, over relatively flat terrain, follows the open shoreline west to Carrying Place Cove, another popular birding spot, before turning inland to reach a subartic heath bog.

From the parking area, explore West Quoddy Head Light, just across South Lubec Road. Commissioned by President Thomas Jefferson, West Quoddy Head Light was first built in 1808. The present tower and house date back to 1858 and were staffed by resident lightkeepers until 1988 when the U.S. Coast Guard installed an automated light. West Quoddy Head's distinct red and white striped exterior set against a background of crashing surf is near postcard perfect; don't forget the camera on this hike.

Leaving West Quoddy Head, cross back over South Lubec Road and walk through the parking area to pick up the Coastal Trail (marked with a sign). Treading along on a dirt path just above the shore for 1.6 miles, you'll reach especially scenic lookouts at Gulliver's Hole and High Ledge (both about 0.3 mile into the hike). At Green Point you'll reach another scenic lookout, about 0.6 mile into the hike; a short spur path leads down onto the pebbled beach. Reaching Carrying Place Cove, the Coastal Trail turns inland and becomes the Thompson Trail. After a 1.1-mile stroll through scrub forest, the Thompson Trail reaches a junction with the Bog Trail. Turn left and follow the boardwalk to this unusual coastal plateau bog; subarctic and arctic plants rarely seen south of Canada are able to grow here in thriving abundance. Shrubs predominate, particularly black crowberry, baked appleberry, and Labrador tea, along with carnivorous plants such as pitcher plants and sundew. Backtrack from the bog to the Thompson Trail and turn left for another 0.4 mile back to the picnic and parking area.

User Groups: Hikers and leashed dogs. No bikes or horses. Wheelchair facilities are limited to the grounds at West Quoddy Head Light.

Permits: A fee of $2 per adult Maine resident or $3 per adult nonresident (age 12 and over) is charged at the state park entrance; senior citizens pay $1 and children under 12 years old enter free. The park season is May 15–October 15, although trailheads are accessible year-round. No staff is on duty and no fee is collected off-season.

Maps: A free trail map, suitable for this hike, is available at the state park entrance. For a topographic map of trails, request Lubec from the USGS.

Directions: From Route 189 in downtown Lubec, turn right on South Lubec Road and follow two miles to a fork, bear left and continue two miles to the park entrance and adjacent picnic area. Handicap parking is available next to the lighthouse visitors center. GPS Coordinates: 44.8167 N, 66.9495 W

Contact: Quoddy Head State Park, 973 South Lubec Rd., Lubec, ME 04652, 207/733-0911, www.maine.gov/doc/parks/index.html.

WESTERN LAKES AND MOUNTAINS

© MIKE SINGER

BEST HIKES

❰ **Backpacking Hikes**
Bigelow Range, **page 91.**
Saddleback Range, **page 97.**
The Mahoosuc Range, **page 108.**

❰ **Bird-Watching**
Mount Agamenticus, **page 119.**

❰ **Summit Hikes**
Saddleback Mountain and The Horn, **page 99.**

❰ **Waterfalls**
Screw Auger Falls, **page 104.**
Step Falls Preserve, **page 105.**

❰ **Wheelchair Access**
Portland: Back Cove Trail and Eastern
   Promenade, **page 118.**

Southernmost Maine is a true microcosm of the state's best natural features. The hikes in this chapter take you to rugged mountains and wild river valleys, densely forested hills, serene lakes, and even a few stops along Maine's jagged ocean coastline. Some of the state's biggest and most popular hiking destinations are here, peaks such as Bigelow Mountain and the summits of the Saddleback Range. Low mountains in the area are no less spectacular, with smaller hills such as Pleasant Mountain and Tumbledown Mountain providing excellent long views for only moderate effort.

Many of the hikes in the western part of the state lie on or very near the Appalachian Trail; others lead to beautiful waterfalls, including Screw Auger Falls and Step Falls, two especially breathtaking cascades in Grafton Notch. The majority of the trails are within minutes of popular tourist areas on Rangeley Lakes and Sebago Lake; even New Hampshire's North Conway makes an easy access point for the Maine continuation of the White Mountain National Forest. And for those seeking truly rugged adventure, Western Maine is a backpacker's paradise and home to some of New England's premier long distance routes, including the 30-mile trek through the Mahoosuc Range.

The southeast coast is dominated by Portland, Maine's largest city. Hikes in this area get you away from the hustle and bustle of the city to catch glimpses of the seacoast's forests, hills, and miles of rocky shoreline. A hidden gem in this area is Vaughn Woods State Park in South Berwick. Here, hundred-year-old trees tower over the shady, pine needle-covered forest floor on this beautiful woods walk along the Salmon River.

At higher elevations and close to the coast, summer temperatures are more moderate than inland locations; but are also less predictable. Inland from the coast, it's blackfly country, with swarms of the pesky insects arriving by June; joined in early July with an equally thick mosquito population. The warm weather hiking season extends into October in the western hills – and into November or even December along the coast. Pine trees and hemlock cover much of this land, but stands of birch still coat the landscape in a golden glow starting in September.

Winter access gets trickier on many of these hikes. In western Maine, some roads, such as Route 113 through Evans Notch, are not maintained in winter, and others simply are often covered with ice and snow. Many of the trails in this part of the state see little or no visitors in winter, meaning you'll probably be breaking trail through snow, without the security of knowing other people might come along to help you out in case of an emergency. That can be exciting, but it's certainly riskier. Along the southeast coast, heavy nor'easter snowstorms and biting wind mark most of the winter months. Still, on the occasional sunny, calm day, walking the Bay Cove Trail in Portland is the best antidote around for a bad case of cabin fever.

A few hikes are on private land left open to public use in keeping with a long-standing tradition in Maine – a state where more than 90 percent of the total land area is privately held. Explore these places with the understanding that you alone are responsible for yourself. Bear in mind that while most of these private-land trails have been open to public use for many years, access can be restricted or denied at any time. Respect private property when on it, obey No Trespassing signs, and assume that hunting is allowed in season unless posted otherwise.

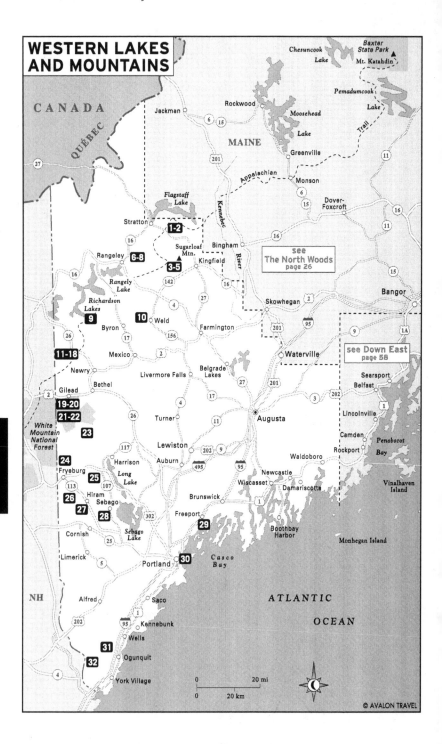

WESTERN LAKES AND MOUNTAINS

◼ BIGELOW RANGE

16.7 mi one-way/2 days

east of Stratton

BEST 《

A darling of Maine hikers, Bigelow Mountain is unquestionably one of the two or three most spectacular peaks in the state; only Katahdin and Bigelow's neighbor to the south, the Saddleback Range, warrant comparison. Reflecting the state's affection for this range, Maine voters supported a grassroots movement and in 1976 created the Bigelow Preserve, a 35,000-acre park encompassing the entire Bigelow Range—including about 17 miles of the Appalachian Trail—and 21 miles of shoreline on sprawling Flagstaff Lake. Both of Bigelow's summits rise well above the tree line, affording long views in every direction. On rare clear days, you can see north to Katahdin and southwest to Mount Washington. This 16.7-mile, two-day backpacking trip traverses the entire Bigelow Mountain range along the Appalachian Trail (AT). The distance is moderate for two days, but don't underestimate the trail's ruggedness.

From East Flagstaff Road, follow the white blazes of the AT southbound, passing a blueblazed side trail at 1.4 miles that leads 0.1 mile to the Little Bigelow lean-to, where there is a good spring and tent space. From there, the AT climbs steadily until cresting the eastern end of the long, low ridge of Little Bigelow Mountain three miles from the road. There are excellent views from open ledges west toward Bigelow Mountain and the ski area at Sugarloaf Mountain, across the Carrabassett Valley. For those looking for a day hike only, this is a logical point of descent (a total roundtrip of six miles).

Dipping back into the forest, the trail then follows the relatively flat, wooded ridge top, passing another open ledge with a view of Bigelow and Flagstaff Lake at 4.5 miles. It then descends about 1,000 feet over less than two miles into Safford Notch, where the forested floor is littered with giant boulders, some of them stacked dramatically atop one another.

At 6.3 miles from East Flagstaff Road, a side trail leads left (southwest) 0.3 mile to tent platforms at the Safford Notch campsite. Just 0.1 mile farther down the AT, the Safford Brook Trail exits right (north), leading 2.2 miles to East Flagstaff Road (and 2.5 miles to Flagstaff Lake). The AT climbs steeply out of Safford Notch, over and around boulders, gaining about 2,000 feet in elevation over two miles to Bigelow's east summit, 4,088-foot Avery Peak. On the way up Avery, the trail passes a side path at 7.5 miles that leads 0.1 mile to an excellent view east and north from atop the cliff called the "Old Man's Head." Beyond that side path, the AT ascends the crest of a narrow, wooded ridge, breaking out of the trees for the final 0.1 mile up Avery Peak. Passing over Avery, the trail descends into the wooded col between the summits, reaching the Avery tenting area at 8.7 miles. There is a water source here, but don't rely on it; by mid-summer, the spring is often dried out.

From the col, the ascent grows fairly steep up West Peak, Bigelow's true summit at 4,145 feet (0.7 mile from Avery Peak). The AT descends to and follows the up-and-down ridge connecting Bigelow to the 3,805-foot summit of South Horn, where you get a good view to the west from directly above Horns Pond. Just 0.1 mile farther, a side trail leads 0.2 mile to the summit of North Horn (3,792 ft.). Continue steeply downhill on the AT, reaching the Horns Pond lean-tos and tent sites at 11.6 miles from East Flagstaff Road and half a mile from South Horn. Horns Pond is a scenic tarn nestled in a tiny bowl at about 3,200 feet on Bigelow's west slope. From here, the AT climbs slightly out of the bowl, passing the junction with the Horns Pond Trail 0.2 mile south of Horns Pond and a short side path to a pond overlook at 0.3 mile. The trail then descends steadily, swinging south and passing the Bigelow Range Trail junction nearly two miles from Horns Pond, to the Cranberry Stream campsite at 14.8 miles (3.2 miles south of Horns Pond and 1.9 miles north of Route 27/16). At 15.8 miles, the AT crosses

Stratton Brook on a bridge before reaching Route 27/16 at mile 16.7 of this trip, 5.1 miles from Horns Pond.

Special note: The traverse of this range ranks among the most popular backpacking treks in New England. Especially during the warmer months, the campsites and shelters fill quickly, even during the week. Bringing a tent is recommended. Also, above the tree line take care to walk only on the trail as fragile alpine vegetation is easily trampled.

Camp at existing camping areas and shelters: Little Bigelow lean-to at 1.4 miles south of East Flagstaff Road, Safford Notch campsite at 6.3 miles, Avery tenting area at 8.7 miles, Horns Pond lean-tos and tent sites at 11.6 miles, and the Cranberry Stream campsite at 14.8 miles.

User Groups: Hikers only. No wheelchair facilities. Dogs are discouraged along the Appalachian Trail in Maine. Bikes and horses are prohibited. This trail should not be attempted in winter except by hikers experienced in mountaineering and prepared for severe winter weather, and is not suitable for skis.

Permits: Parking, access, and camping are free. Backcountry camping accommodations are available on a first-come, first-served basis.

Maps: A free contour map of trails in the Bigelow Preserve is available at some trailheads and from the Maine Bureau of Public Lands. Detailed trail maps are available from the Maine Appalachian Club (Kennebec River to Maine Highway 27, $8) and the Appalachian Mountain Club (Rangeley–Stratton/Baxter State Park–Katahdin, $7.95 in waterproof Tyvek). For topographic area maps, request Little Bigelow Mountain, the Horns, Sugarloaf Mountain, and Poplar Mountain from the USGS.

Directions: You need to shuttle two vehicles for this trip. To do the hike from north to south, as described here, leave one vehicle at the junction of the Appalachian Trail and Routes 27 and 16, 5.3 miles south of where Routes 27 and 16 split in Stratton and 16

miles north of where Routes 27 and 16 split in Kingfield. Then drive on Route 16 east to North New Portland. Turn left (north) in front of the country store onto Long Falls Dam Road and follow it for 17.4 miles. Bear left onto the dirt Bog Brook Road. Drive 0.7 mile, bear left onto the dirt East Flagstaff Road, and drive 0.1 mile. Park either in the gravel pit on the right or at the roadside where the Appalachian Trail crosses the road just beyond the pit.

GPS Coordinates: 45.1361 N, 70.1597 W

Contact: Maine Department of Conservation, Bureau of Parks and Lands, 286 Water St., Key Bank Plaza, 3rd and 5th floors, Augusta, ME 04333-0022, 207/287-3821, www.state. me.us/doc/parks. Maine Appalachian Trail Club, P.O. Box 283, Augusta, ME 04332-0283, www.matc.org. Appalachian Mountain Club, 5 Joy St., Boston, MA 02108, 617/523-0655, www.outdoors.org. For information about a hiker shuttle, free Kennebec River ferry service, and other hiker services along the Appalachian Trail in Maine, contact Steve Longley, P.O. Box 90, Rte. 201, The Forks, ME 04985, 207/663-4441, 207/246-4642, or 888/356-2863 (in Maine only), www.riversandtrails.com.

☑ BIGELOW MOUNTAIN
13.8 mi/10.5 hr or 1-2 days
🥾5 ⛰10

east of Stratton

This hike up one of Maine's most spectacular and popular mountains, Bigelow, can be accomplished in a single long day by fit hikers getting an early start. But there are two camping areas along the trail that offer the option of a two-day trip, leaving your heavy pack behind for the day hike to Bigelow's summits. The cumulative elevation gained by hitting both of Bigelow's summits is nearly 4,000 feet, much of it above the tree line. Dress appropriately for rapidly changing weather conditions and stick to the trail to avoid trampling fragile alpine vegetation.

For the Bigelow summit hike, begin at Stratton Brook Pond Road and follow the white blazes of the Appalachian Trail (AT) northbound into the woods. Within a quarter mile you will cross a logging road and Stratton Brook on a bridge. The AT ascends steadily, passing the Cranberry Stream campsite at 1.1 miles and a junction with the Bigelow Range Trail at 2.4 miles. Stay on the AT, which swings east and climbs past a short side trail out to ledges above Horns Pond at four miles, and then passes the Horns Pond Trail junction 0.1 mile farther. The trail drops slightly into the bowl, home to the tiny mountain tarn called Horns Pond and a camping area with two lean-tos and tent sites, at 4.3 miles.

The AT climbs steeply for the next half mile, passing a side trail leading 0.2 mile to North Horn (3,792 ft.) at 4.7 miles and reaching the South Horn summit (3,805 ft.) at 4.8 miles, with a good view over Horns Pond and north to Flagstaff Lake. Descending steeply off South Horn, you follow an up-and-down ridge for more than a mile. Then climb steeply to West Peak, Bigelow's true summit at 4,145 feet, 6.9 miles in. The rocky, open summit affords views in every direction: north over Flagstaff Lake and the wilderness of the North Woods, all the way to Katahdin on a clear day, and southwest to Mount Washington when conditions are right. For this hike, turn around and descend the same way you came. To reach 4,088-foot Avery Peak, continue northbound on the AT, dropping into the saddle between Bigelow's two summits, passing the Avery tenting area at 7.2 miles, and then climbing to the open summit of Avery Peak. Hiking to Avery and back adds 1.4 miles and an hour (possibly more) to this hike's distance.

Special note: To make a loop hike of about 12.5 miles instead of this route over Bigelow's two summits, go up the Fire Warden's Trail, which begins a little more than a half mile beyond the Appalachian Trail crossing of Stratton Brook Pond Road. Climb the Fire Warden's Trail for 3.5 miles to Avery col, turn right (northbound) on the AT for 0.4 mile to Avery Peak, then turn around and descend the AT southbound for nearly eight miles to Stratton Brook Road. Turn left and walk the road for 0.5 mile to complete the loop. The upper half mile of the Fire Warden's Trail is very steep and severely eroded.

Camp at existing camping areas and shelters, which along this route include the Cranberry Stream campsite 1.1 miles from Stratton Brook Pond Road, the Horns Pond lean-tos and tent sites at 4.3 miles, and the Avery tenting area at 7.2 miles. Bigelow Mountain ranks among the most popular peaks in New England. Especially during the warmer months, the campsites and shelters fill quickly, even during the week. Bringing a tent is recommended.

User Groups: Hikers only. Bikes and horses are prohibited; no wheelchair facilities. Dogs are discouraged along the Appalachian Trail in Maine. This trail should not be attempted in winter except by hikers experienced in mountaineering and prepared for severe winter weather, and is not suitable for skis.

Permits: Parking, access, and camping are free. Backcountry camping accommodations are available on a first-come, first-served basis.

Maps: A free contour map of trails in the Bigelow Preserve is available at some trailheads and from the Maine Bureau of Public Lands. Detailed trail maps are available from the Maine Appalachian Club (Kennebec River to Maine Highway 27, $8) and the Appalachian Mountain Club (Rangeley–Stratton/Baxter State Park–Katahdin, $7.95 in waterproof Tyvek). For topographic area maps, request Horns and Sugarloaf Mountain from the USGS.

Directions: From the intersection of Routes 27 and 16 in Stratton (where the two roads join), drive east on Route 27/16 for approximately five miles to Stratton Brook Pond Road. Turn left (north) and drive 1.4 miles to where the AT crosses the dirt road; park at the roadside.

GPS Coordinates: 45.1097 N, 70.3636 W

Contact: Maine Department of Conservation, Bureau of Parks and Lands, 286 Water St., Key Bank Plaza, 3rd and 5th floors, Augusta, ME 04333-0022, 207/287-3821, www.state.me.us/doc/parks. Maine Appalachian Trail Club, P.O. Box 283, Augusta, ME 04332-0283, www.matc.org. Appalachian Mountain Club, 5 Joy St., Boston, MA 02108, 617/523-0655, www.outdoors.org.

🖪 SUGARLOAF MOUNTAIN
5.8 mi/4.5 hr   🏃5 ⛰9

south of Stratton

Maine's third-highest peak at 4,237 feet, Sugarloaf's barren summit offers long views in every direction. On a clear day, you can see Mount Washington in New Hampshire to the southwest and all the way to Katahdin in the far north. Like any high, exposed peak, this can be a rough place in foul weather: prepare for the possibility of swirling fog and biting wind, even when conditions at the trailhead are hot and sunny. Sugarloaf Mountain is also one of Maine's most popular downhill ski areas. But this day hike of Sugarloaf, via the Appalachian Trail (AT), is a rugged, 5.8-mile route that shows very little evidence of the resort. It's only when you reach the summit that you see a cluster of ski area buildings. The climb's net elevation gain is approximately 2,000 feet.

From Caribou Valley Road, follow the white-blazed AT to the left (south), immediately crossing the South Branch of the Carrabassett River, which can be dangerous at times of high water. The AT then climbs very steeply up Sugarloaf Mountain, involving short stretches of tricky scrambling up a heavily eroded trail. The trail emerges from the woods high on the north slope of Sugarloaf, with views to South and North Crocker across the valley. It reenters the woods and then reaches a junction with the Sugarloaf Mountain Trail 2.3 miles from Caribou Valley Road. Turn left onto that trail and follow its rocky path steeply uphill for 0.6 mile to the exposed Sugarloaf summit, where there are ski area buildings and long views in every direction. Descend the same route back to the road.

Special note: Sugarloaf can be linked with Spaulding Mountain by continuing on the AT southbound, a 10.2-mile round-trip from Caribou Valley Road. An ambitious hiker can continue on to Mount Abraham, making a 17.4-mile day hike or a two-day backpacking trip. (See *Spaulding Mountain* and *Mount Abraham* listings in this chapter for more details.)

User Groups: Hikers only. Bikes and horses are prohibited; no wheelchair facilities. Dogs are discouraged along the Appalachian Trail in Maine. Access to this trail by car during the winter may be limited since Caribou Valley Road may not be plowed; however, it could be skied as far as the AT crossing. Hiking Sugarloaf should not be attempted in winter except by hikers experienced in mountaineering and prepared for severe winter weather.

Permits: Parking, access, and camping are free. Backcountry camping accommodations are available on a first-come, first-served basis.

Maps: Detailed trail maps are available from the Maine Appalachian Club (Maine Highway 27 to Maine Highway 17, $8) and the Appalachian Mountain Club (Rangeley–Stratton/Baxter State Park–Katahdin, $7.95 in waterproof Tyvek). For a topographic area map, request Sugarloaf Mountain from the USGS.

Directions: From Route 27/16 in Bigelow (listed on some maps as Carrabassett), about a mile west of the entrance to the Sugarloaf USA ski resort, turn south (left) onto the dirt Caribou Valley Road. Drive 4.3 miles to the Appalachian Trail crossing and park at the roadside. The dirt Caribou Valley Road was improved in recent years all the way to the AT crossing and is now passable for cars during the warm months.

GPS Coordinates: 45.0808 N, 70.3394 W
Contact: Maine Appalachian Trail Club, P.O. Box 283, Augusta, ME 04332-0283, www. matc.org. Appalachian Mountain Club, 5 Joy St., Boston, MA 02108, 617/523-0655, www. outdoors.org.

4 SPAULDING MOUNTAIN
9 mi/7 hr
🚶5 ⛰8

south of Stratton

At 4,010 feet, Spaulding offers good—if not spectacular—views towards neighboring Sugarloaf Mountain and Mount Abraham. Reaching Spaulding actually requires a partial climb up Sugarloaf and the best feature on this hike may be the route's fairly flat ridge walk from Sugarloaf to Spaulding, a quiet stretch of trail through a lush forest of hemlock, ferns, and moss. Keep quiet and watch for wildlife here—one intrepid hiker tells of running into a bull moose with a 26-point rack while out on Spaulding one crisp day in fall. He and his companions estimated the antlers spanned nearly six feet. The total elevation on this hike is slightly more than 2,000 feet.

From Caribou Valley Road, turn left (south) on the AT, immediately crossing the South Branch of the Carrabassett River, which can be dangerous at times of high water. The trail climbs very steeply up Sugarloaf Mountain, involving short stretches of tricky scrambling on a heavily eroded trail. It breaks out of the woods high on Sugarloaf's north slope, with views to South and North Crocker across the valley. It reenters the woods and then reaches a junction with the Sugarloaf Mountain Trail, 2.3 miles from Caribou Valley Road. From the Sugarloaf Mountain Trail junction, follow the AT along the fairly flat ridge from Sugarloaf to Spaulding. About 0.1 mile south of the Sugarloaf Mountain Trail junction, a side path leads about 40 feet to a good view. The AT continues along the wooded ridge to a junction with the Spaulding Mountain

Trail, 4.4 miles from Caribou Valley Road. That trail leads 0.1 mile uphill to Spaulding's summit. Return the way you came.

The Spaulding Mountain lean-to is located down a short side path off the AT, 5.2 miles south of Caribou Valley Road and 0.8 mile south of the Spaulding Mountain Trail/Appalachian Trail junction.

User Groups: Hikers only. Bikes and horses are prohibited; no wheelchair facilities. Dogs are discouraged along the Appalachian Trail in Maine.

Permits: Parking, access, and camping are free. Backcountry camping accommodations are available on a first-come, first-served basis.

Maps: Detailed trail maps are available from the Maine Appalachian Club (Maine Highway 27 to Maine Highway 17, $8) and the Appalachian Mountain Club (Rangeley–Stratton/Baxter State Park–Katahdin, $7.95 in waterproof Tyvek). For a topographic area map, request Sugarloaf Mountain from the USGS.

Directions: From Route 27/16, about a mile west of the entrance to the Sugarloaf USA ski resort in Bigelow (also listed as Carrabassett on some maps), turn left (south) onto the dirt Caribou Valley Road. Drive 4.3 miles to the Appalachian Trail crossing and park at the roadside. The dirt Caribou Valley Road was improved in recent years all the way to the AT crossing.

GPS Coordinates: 45.0808 N, 70.3394 W
Contact: Maine Appalachian Trail Club, P.O. Box 283, Augusta, ME 04332-0283, www. matc.org. Appalachian Mountain Club, 5 Joy St., Boston, MA 02108, 617/523-0655, www. outdoors.org.

5 MOUNT ABRAHAM
16 mi/12 hr or 1-2 days
🚶5 ⛰10

south of Stratton

Mount Abraham boasts one of the largest alpine areas in Maine, with more than four miles of ridge above the tree line featuring excellent panoramic views. But because Appalachian Trail (AT) hikers have to make a 3.4-mile detour to climb Abraham, it attracts fewer visitors than some peaks in western Maine, such as neighboring Saddleback Mountain. This 16-mile hike to bag one of Maine's 14 4,000-footers is difficult and long—a conceivable one-day goal for fit hikers getting an early start at a time of year that affords lots of daylight, but it also makes for a satisfying two-day trip in relative solitude. The cumulative elevation gain on the round-trip is about 3,200 feet.

From Caribou Valley Road, turn left (southbound) on the AT, immediately crossing the South Branch of the Carrabassett River, which can be dangerous at times of high water. The trail then climbs very steeply up Sugarloaf Mountain, involving short stretches of tricky scrambling up a heavily eroded trail. The trail emerges from the woods high on the north slope of Sugarloaf, with views to South and North Crocker across the valley. It reenters the woods and then reaches a junction with the Sugarloaf Mountain Trail 2.3 miles from Caribou Valley Road. (For a scenic 1.2-mile detour off this hike, follow that rocky trail steeply uphill to the exposed 4,237-foot Sugarloaf summit, Maine's third-highest peak, where there are ski area buildings and long views in every direction.) From the Sugarloaf Mountain Trail junction, follow the AT along the fairly flat ridge that connects Sugarloaf to Spaulding Mountain—a quiet stretch through a lush forest of hemlock, ferns, and moss. About 0.1 mile south of the Sugarloaf Mountain Trail junction, a side path leads some 40 feet to a good view. The AT continues along the wooded ridge to a junction with the Spaulding Mountain Trail, 4.4 miles from Caribou Valley Road. (That trail, which is not included in this hike's distance, leads 0.1 mile uphill to Spaulding's 4,010-foot summit, where three short side paths lead to limited views toward Sugarloaf and Abraham.) From the Spaulding Mountain Trail junction, the AT descends 0.8 mile to a side path leading 150 feet to the Spaulding Mountain lean-to, where there is space for tents.

The AT follows moderate terrain southward, reaching the Mount Abraham Trail 1.1 miles from the Spaulding lean-to. On this blue-blazed trail, it's 1.7 miles one-way to Abraham's 4,043-foot summit. Although it's relatively flat for the first half mile, the trail—after emerging from the woods—climbs over three bumps on a ridge, crossing rough talus slopes. From the summit, marked by the rusting remains of an old fire tower, the Horn and Saddleback Mountain are visible to the southwest, and the Bigelow Range can be seen to the north. About 30 feet from the tower, along the Fire Warden's Trail, there is a primitive stone shelter with a shingled roof and enough space under its very low ceiling for a few people to crawl inside; not a very roomy spot, but good for an emergency shelter. About 100 feet beyond the summit stand several tall cairns. For this hike, return to Caribou Valley Road via the same route you took up.

The Spaulding Mountain lean-to is located down a short side path off the AT, 5.2 miles south of Caribou Valley Road.

User Groups: Hikers only. Bikes and horses are prohibited; no wheelchair facilities. Dogs are discouraged along the Appalachian Trail in Maine. The Caribou Valley Road may not be plowed in winter to provide access to this trail, though it could be skied as far as the AT crossing. Hiking Abraham should not be attempted in winter except by hikers experienced in mountaineering and prepared for severe winter weather.

Permits: Parking, access, and camping are free. Backcountry camping accommodations are available on a first-come, first-served basis.

Maps: Detailed trail maps are available from the Maine Appalachian Club (Maine Highway 27 to Maine Highway 17, $8) and the Appalachian Mountain Club (Rangeley–Stratton/Baxter State Park–Katahdin, $7.95 in waterproof Tyvek). For topographic area maps, request Sugarloaf Mountain and Mount Abraham from the USGS.

Directions: From Route 27/16, about a mile west of the entrance to the Sugarloaf USA ski resort in Bigelow (also listed as Carrabassett on some maps), turn left (south) onto the dirt Caribou Valley Road. Drive 4.3 miles to the Appalachian Trail crossing and park at the roadside. The dirt Caribou Valley Road was improved in recent years all the way to the AT crossing and is now passable for cars during the warm months.

GPS Coordinates: 45.0808 N, 70.3394 W

Contact: Maine Appalachian Trail Club, P.O. Box 283, Augusta, ME 04332-0283, www.matc.org. Appalachian Mountain Club, 5 Joy St., Boston, MA 02108, 617/523-0655, www.outdoors.org.

6 SADDLEBACK RANGE
32.2 mi one-way/3-4 days
🏃5 ⛰10

east of Rangeley

BEST (

The Saddleback Range stands out as one of the three premier mountain ranges in Maine—the other two being the greater Katahdin region and the Bigelow Range—and a multiday traverse of its peaks is as rugged, varied, and scenic a mountain experience as can be had anywhere in New England. Seven of the eight summits rise above 4,000 feet, and four of them thrust extensive areas above the tree line, offering long, panoramic views. Three miles of ridge above the trees extend from Saddleback Mountain to the Horn. Wintry storms with dangerously high winds occur year-round, so avoid this exposed ground if bad weather threatens. This traverse could be accomplished in three days. If you allow time to make the side trips to Sugarloaf Mountain and Mount Abraham, you are likely to be out on the trail for four days. Both side trips add to this hike's 32.2-mile distance.

From Route 16/27, follow the white blazes of the Appalachian Trail southbound. It rises gently at first and never grows more than moderately steep before reaching the wooded North Crocker Mountain summit (4,168 ft.), 5.2 miles from the highway. There are limited views over the tops of low spruce trees. A better view is along the AT just south of the

nearing the summit of Saddleback Mountain

© KD TALBOT/WWW.GHOSTFLOWERS.COM

summit, looking toward Sugarloaf Mountain and Mount Abraham. Continuing south on the AT, you drop into the shallow col between the two summits of Crocker, then climb to the top of South Crocker (4,010 ft.), a mile away from North Crocker. The actual summit is reached via a 100-foot side path off the AT. An open ledge there affords a limited view toward Sugarloaf and Abraham.

Descending south, the AT crosses an open slope of loose, broken rocks with views north and east toward the Bigelow Range. Footing becomes difficult descending the steep and very loose final half mile to Crocker Cirque campsite, just over a mile from South Crocker's summit and 7.3 miles from Route 27/16. One mile farther south, the AT crosses the dirt Caribou Valley Road (which was improved in recent years all the way to the AT crossing, providing another access to the AT; Route 16/27 is 4.3 miles down Caribou Valley Road). From the road, the AT immediately crosses the South Branch of the Carrabassett River—which can be dangerous at times of high water—then climbs very steeply up Sugarloaf Mountain, involving short stretches of tricky scrambling. The trail emerges from the woods high on Sugarloaf's north slope, with views of the Crockers across the valley. It reenters the woods and then reaches a junction with the Sugarloaf Mountain Trail 3.3 miles south of Crocker Cirque campsite (and 2.3 miles from Caribou Valley Road); this rocky trail leads steeply uphill 0.6 mile to the exposed 4,237-foot Sugarloaf summit, Maine's third-highest peak, where there are ski area buildings and long views in every direction. From the Sugarloaf Mountain Trail junction, the AT follows the fairly flat ridge connecting Sugarloaf to Spaulding Mountain—a quiet trail stretch through a lush forest of hemlock, ferns, and moss. About 0.1 mile south of the Sugarloaf Mountain Trail junction, a side path leads about 40 feet to a good view. The AT continues along the wooded ridge to a junction with the Spaulding Mountain Trail, 5.4 miles from Crocker Cirque campsite; this trail leads 0.1

mile uphill to Spaulding's 4,010-foot summit, where three short side paths lead to limited views toward Sugarloaf and Abraham.

From the Spaulding Mountain Trail junction, the AT descends 0.8 mile to a side path leading 150 feet to the Spaulding Mountain lean-to, where there is also space for tents. The AT follows moderate terrain south, reaching the Mount Abraham Trail 1.1 miles from the Spaulding lean-to. On this blue-blazed trail, it's 1.7 miles one-way to the 4,043-foot Abraham summit. Although it's relatively flat for the first half mile, after emerging from the woods, the trail climbs over three bumps on a ridge, crossing talus slopes reminiscent of bigger mountains like Washington or Katahdin. The views from Abraham are among the best in the range. From the Mount Abraham Trail junction, the AT southbound passes a view toward Abraham within 0.2 mile and then passes over the wooded top of Lone Mountain in a mile.

Descending, the trail follows and then crosses beautiful Perham Stream (immediately after crossing a logging road), its narrow current choked with moss-covered rocks. The AT crosses a second logging road and, 1.2 miles from Perham Stream, crosses another gem, Sluice Brook, which parallels the trail for 0.7 mile before pouring through a narrow flume. The trail crosses a gravel road and descends very steeply to Orbeton Stream, 5.3 miles from the Spaulding lean-to; fording can be difficult in high water. From Orbeton, the AT makes one of its steepest and most arduous ascents in this range, more than two miles to the open ledges of Poplar Ridge, where there are views to the south and east. A half mile beyond the ledges is the Poplar Ridge lean-to (a small brook provides water, but may be dried out by late summer).

From the shelter, the AT climbs steadily 1.4 miles to the open summit of Saddleback Junior (3,655 ft.), with excellent views in all directions. Follow white blazes and cairns across the Saddleback Junior top, descend about 500 feet, and then climb steeply 1,000 feet to the open, 4,041-foot summit of the Horn, two miles from Saddleback Junior. Again the views are spectacular, encompassing the Rangeley Lake area and Saddleback Mountain to the west, and extending north to Katahdin and southwest to Washington on a clear day.

Descend south on the AT, crossing mostly open ground with nonstop views, and then ascend Saddleback's ledges to the lower of its two summits. Walk the easy ridge to the true summit, at 4,120 feet, 1.6 miles from the Horn's summit. Continuing south, the AT drops back into the woods a mile below the summit and then crosses a logging road nearly a mile below the tree line. The trail crosses a stream 0.2 mile beyond the logging road and crosses Saddleback Stream 0.6 mile farther. At 3.7 miles from Saddleback's summit, a side path leads a short distance to the Caves, actually passageways through giant boulders that have cleaved from the cliff above over the eons. Just 0.2 mile past the Caves, the trail reaches the Piazza Rock lean-to area, a popular backcountry campsite less than two miles from Route 4. There are tent sites and a large shelter, but this place fills quickly on weekends. A side path off the AT leads about 200 yards uphill to Piazza Rock, an enormous horizontal slab protruding improbably from the cliff. You can follow the trail up onto the slab with a little scrambling. From the lean-to area, the AT descends south for 1.8 miles to Route 4, this hike's terminus.

There are three lean-to shelters and one campsite along this section of the Appalachian Trail: the Crocker Cirque campsite, with three tent platforms, lies 0.1 mile down a side path off the AT, 7.3 miles south of Route 27/16; the Spaulding Mountain lean-to is located down a short side path off the AT, 6.2 miles south of the Crocker Cirque campsite; the Poplar Ridge lean-to sits along the AT, eight miles south of the Spaulding Mountain lean-to; and the Piazza Rock lean-to lies on a short side path off the AT, 8.9 miles south of the Poplar Ridge lean-to.

User Groups: Hikers only. Bikes and horses are prohibited; no wheelchair facilities. Dogs are discouraged along the Appalachian Trail in Maine. This trail should not be attempted in winter except by hikers experienced in mountaineering and prepared for severe winter weather, and is not suitable for skis.

Permits: Parking, access, and camping are free. Backcountry camping accommodations are available on a first-come, first-served basis.

Maps: Detailed trail maps are available from the Maine Appalachian Club (Maine Highway 27 to Maine Highway 17, $8) and the Appalachian Mountain Club (Rangeley–Stratton/Baxter State Park–Katahdin, $7.95 in waterproof Tyvek). For topographic area maps, request Sugarloaf Mountain, Black Nubble, Mount Abraham, Redington, and Saddleback Mountain from the USGS.

Directions: You need to shuttle two vehicles for this backpacking trip. To do the hike from north to south, as described here, leave one vehicle where the Appalachian Trail crosses Route 4, about 12 miles north of the junction of Routes 4 and 142 in Phillips and 10.1 miles south of the junction of Routes 4 and 16. Then drive to the hike's start, where the AT crosses Route 27/16, 5.3 miles east of where Routes 27 and 16 join in Stratton and 16 miles west of where Routes 27 and 16 split in Kingfield. GPS Coordinates: 45.1035 N, 70.3556 W

Contact: Maine Appalachian Trail Club, P.O. Box 283, Augusta, ME 04332-0283, www.matc.org. Appalachian Mountain Club, 5 Joy St., Boston, MA 02108, 617/523-0655, www.outdoors.org. For information about a hiker shuttle and other hiker services along the Appalachian Trail in Maine, contact Steve Longley, P.O. Box 90, Rte. 201, The Forks, ME 04985, 207/663-4441 or 888/356-2863 (in Maine only), www.riversandtrails.com.

🛚 SADDLEBACK MOUNTAIN AND THE HORN

13.4 mi/8.5 hr   🏃5   ⛰10

southeast of Rangeley

BEST (

Saddleback Mountain rises to 4,120 feet, offering some of the best views in the state from its summit and from the open, three-mile ridge linking it and its neighboring 4,000-footer, the Horn. A round-trip hike on the Appalachian Trail (AT) from Route 4 to the true Saddleback summit—the first of its two summits reached from this direction—is a strenuous 10.2-mile day hike. Continuing to the Horn makes the round-trip distance a very challenging 13.4 miles, with a cumulative 3,800 feet of uphill. Although these are among the most sought-after Maine summits, avoid this exposed ridge in inclement weather. Also carry plenty of water, as there is no water source above the outlet to Moose and Deer Pond.

From Route 4, follow the white blazes of the AT northbound. Within 0.1 mile, the trail crosses a bridge over Sandy River and then climbs steadily to the Piazza Rock lean-to and camping area, 1.8 miles from the road (a very popular destination among weekend backpackers). A side path off the AT leads about 200 yards uphill to Piazza Rock, an enormous horizontal slab protruding improbably from the cliff. You can follow the trail up onto the slab with a little scrambling. Following the AT 0.2 mile north of the camping area, pass another side path leading a short distance to the Caves, actually passageways through giant boulders that have cleaved from the cliff above over the eons. Just over a mile beyond the Caves side path, the AT crosses Saddleback Stream, and 0.6 mile farther it crosses the Moose and Deer Pond outlet, the last water source on this hike. At 4.7 miles from Route 4, the trail emerges above the tree line on Saddleback and ascends the open ridge another mile to the summit. Views here are spectacular, encompassing the Rangeley Lake area to the west, the Horn to the northeast, and extending north to Katahdin and southwest to Washington on a clear day. The AT continues down into the slight saddle that gives the mountain its name, over Saddleback's second summit, and then drops more steeply over ledges for several hundred feet into the col between Saddleback and the Horn. It turns upward again, climbing gently to the 4,041-foot summit of the Horn, 1.6

miles from Saddleback's summit, where again the views are long in every direction. The AT continues north, but this hike returns via the same route you came.

The Piazza Rock lean-to and camping area is reached via a short side path off the Appalachian Trail, 1.8 miles north of Route 4.

User Groups: Hikers only. Bikes and horses are prohibited; no wheelchair facilities. Dogs are discouraged along the Appalachian Trail in Maine. This trail should not be attempted in winter except by hikers experienced in mountaineering and prepared for severe winter weather, and is not suitable for skis.

Permits: Parking, access, and camping are free. Backcountry camping accommodations are available on a first-come, first-served basis.

Maps: Detailed trail maps are available from the Maine Appalachian Club (Maine Highway 27 to Maine Highway 17, $8) and the Appalachian Mountain Club (Rangeley–Stratton/Baxter State Park–Katahdin, $7.95 in waterproof Tyvek). For topographic area maps, request Redington and Saddleback Mountain from the USGS.

Directions: Park in the roadside turnout where the AT crosses Route 4, about 12 miles north of the junction of Routes 4 and 142 in Phillips and 10.1 miles south of the junction of Routes 4 and 16 in Rangeley.

GPS Coordinates: 44.8910 N, 70.5371 W

Contact: Maine Appalachian Trail Club, P.O. Box 283, Augusta, ME 04332-0283, www.matc.org. Appalachian Mountain Club, 5 Joy St., Boston, MA 02108, 617/523-0655, www.outdoors.org.

8 PIAZZA ROCK AND THE CAVES

4 mi/3 hr

southeast of Rangeley

Many Appalachian Trail (AT) hikers continue beyond Piazza Rock and the Caves on their way to bag Saddleback Mountain and the Horn. But these two interesting geological formations just a couple miles from the road offer a wonderful destination for a short hike that climbs little more than a few hundred feet—it's especially suited for children. Piazza Rock is an enormous horizontal slab protruding improbably from the cliff. The Caves are interesting passageways through giant boulders that have cleaved from the cliff above over the eons. The lean-to and camping area nearby provides the option of an overnight trip, though the area is very popular and fills quickly on summer and fall weekends.

From Route 4, follow the white blazes of the AT northbound. Within 0.1 mile, the trail crosses a bridge over Sandy River and then climbs steadily to the Piazza Rock lean-to, 1.8 miles from the highway. Turn left on a side path that leads about 200 yards uphill to Piazza Rock. You can follow the trail up onto the slab with a little scrambling. Returning to the AT, follow the trail another 0.2 mile north to a short spur path leading to the Caves. Hike back to your vehicle the same way you came.

The Piazza Rock lean-to and camping area is reached via a short side path off the Appalachian Trail, 1.8 miles north of Route 4.

User Groups: Hikers only. Bikes and horses are prohibited; no wheelchair facilities. Dogs are discouraged along the Appalachian Trail in Maine. This trail is not suitable for skis.

Permits: Parking, access, and camping are free. Backcountry camping accommodations are available on a first-come, first-served basis.

Maps: Detailed trail maps are available from the Maine Appalachian Club (Maine Highway 27 to Maine Highway 17, $8) and the Appalachian Mountain Club (Rangeley–Stratton/Baxter State Park–Katahdin, $7.95 in waterproof Tyvek). For topographic area maps, request Redington and Saddleback Mountain from the USGS.

Directions: Park in the roadside turnout where the AT crosses Route 4, about 12 miles north of the junction of Routes 4 and 142 in Phillips and 10.1 miles south of the junction of Routes 4 and 16 in Rangeley.

GPS Coordinates: 44.8910 N, 70.5371 W

Contact: Maine Appalachian Trail Club, P.O. Box 283, Augusta, ME 04332-0283, www.matc.org. Appalachian Mountain Club, 5 Joy St., Boston, MA 02108, 617/523-0655, www.outdoors.org.

9 OLD BLUE MOUNTAIN

5.6 mi/4 hr   🏃5 ⛰9

north of Andover

From the first steps up this remote stretch of the Appalachian Trail (AT) to the dazzling 360 degree views atop the 3,600-foot summit of Old Blue Mountain, this is a hike without a dull moment. Moose travel freely through the hardwood forest here, and, without the heavy boot traffic on the trail, you might even see the reclusive black bear lumbering nearby—or at least come across scat and prints. The best time to hike Old Blue is between July and early October—but be prepared for any type of weather. Even in late May and early June, the mountain's weather can feel more like March. The elevation gain is about 2,200 feet.

The AT leaves South Arm Road (look for a sign a few steps in from the road) and its first mile climbs steeply above spectacular Black Brook Notch. Atop the cliffs, watch for an open ledge to the trail's right with an unobstructed view of the notch. At approximately two miles out from the trailhead, the AT then meanders to the summit through dense woods, at one point offering a good view toward Old Blue's summit. The summit itself is a broad plateau covered with scrub trees and offering views in all directions. Visible to the south are the Mahoosucs and the slopes of the Sunday River Ski Area; to the northeast are the Saddleback Range and Bigelow Mountain. Descend the same way you came.

User Groups: Hikers only. Bikes and horses

are prohibited; no wheelchair facilities. Dogs are discouraged along the Appalachian Trail in Maine. This trail should not be attempted in winter except by hikers experienced in mountaineering and prepared for severe winter weather, and is not suitable for skis.

Permits: Parking, access, and camping are free. Backcountry camping accommodations are available on a first-come, first-served basis.

Maps: A detailed trail map of this portion of the Appalachian Trail is available from the Maine Appalachian Club (Maine Highway 17 to Maine–New Hampshire State Line,$8). For topographic area maps, request Metallak Mountain and Andover from the USGS.

Directions: From the junction of Routes 5 and 120 in Andover, head east on Route 120 for half a mile and then turn left onto South Arm Road. Drive another 7.7 miles into Black Brook Notch to where the AT crosses the road. Park at the roadside.

GPS Coordinates: 44.7219 N, 70.7856 W

Contact: Maine Appalachian Trail Club, P.O. Box 283, Augusta, ME 04332-0283, www. matc.org. Appalachian Trail Conference, 799 Washington St., P.O. Box 807, Harpers Ferry, WV 25425-0807, 304/535-6331, www.appalachiantrail.org.

🔟 TUMBLEDOWN MOUNTAIN BROOK TRAIL

3.8 mi/3 hr   4 ⛰️ 10

northwest of Weld

With a 700-foot cliff on its south face, a pristine alpine pond, and more than a half mile of open, rocky ridge, Tumbledown Mountain seems far taller than 3,068 feet. The views from the ridge and two peaks (East and West) take in a landscape of mountains and lakes offering few, if any, signs of human presence. The long views stretch far to the east, south, and west, all the way to Mount Washington and the White Mountains in New Hampshire

(the tall ridge looming in the distance to the southwest). There are other trails to the top of Tumbledown, but this one is significantly easier and more appropriate for children and casual hikers, though it still climbs approximately 1,900 feet. All trail junctions are marked with signs.

From the parking area, the Brook Trail follows an old logging road for its first mile and then climbs more steeply for the next half mile to Tumbledown Pond, a scenic alpine tarn tucked amid Tumbledown's three summits (East, West, and North Peaks). From the pond, turn left (west) on the Tumbledown Ridge Trail and hike up a moderately steep, open ridge of rock for 0.4 mile to East Peak, where there are sweeping mountain views to the east, south, and west, all the way to Mount Washington.

This hike ends here and returns the way you came. But to reach West Peak—the true summit at 3,068 feet—follow the Tumbledown Ridge Trail another 0.3 mile west; it drops down into the saddle between the peaks and then climbs the rocky ridge to West Peak (adding 0.6 mile to this hike's distance).

User Groups: Hikers and dogs. Not suitable for bikes or horses; no wheelchair facilities.

Permits: Parking and access are free.

Maps: For a contour map of trails, obtain the Camden–Pleasant–Weld/Mahoosuc–Evans map, $7.95 in waterproof Tyvek, from the Appalachian Mountain Club. For topographic area maps, request Weld, Madrid, Roxbury, and Jackson Mountain from the USGS.

Directions: From the junction of Routes 142 and 156 in Weld, drive 2.4 miles north on Route 142 to Weld Corner. Turn left onto West Side Road at the Mount Blue State Park sign. Continue a half mile and bear right on a dirt road. Drive 2.3 miles on that road, passing the Mountain View Cemetery, and then bear right again on another dirt road, heading toward Byron Notch. From that intersection, it's 1.6 miles to the Brook Trail; park at the roadside.

Contact: Tumbledown Conservation Alliance, P.O. Box 24, Weld, ME 04285, www.

tumbledown.org. Appalachian Mountain Club, 5 Joy St., Boston, MA 02108, 617/523-0655, www.outdoors.org.

11 TABLE ROCK, GRAFTON NOTCH

2.5 mi/1.5 hr

in Grafton Notch State Park

Flanked to the south by Old Speck Mountain and to the north by Baldpate Mountain, Grafton Notch takes a deep bite out of this western Maine stretch of the Appalachians and marks the northern terminus of the Mahoosuc Range. Perched hundreds of feet up Baldpate Mountain, the broad, flat Table Rock overlooks the notch. Visible from Route 26, Baldpate affords commanding views of the notch and Old Speck. This 2.5-mile loop over Table Rock employs the Appalachian Trail and the orange-blazed Table Rock Trail, which ascends very steeply and relentlessly for a mile. The vertical ascent above Grafton Notch is nearly 1,000 feet.

From the parking lot, pick up the white-blazed Appalachian Trail (AT) heading north, crossing the highway. After reentering the woods, follow the AT for 0.1 mile and then turn right at the sign for Table Rock. The orange-blazed trail almost immediately grows steep, emerging a mile later at the so-called slab caves, which are actually intriguing cavities amid boulders rather than true caves. The trail turns right and circles around and up onto Table Rock. To descend, walk off the back of Table Rock, following a blue-blazed trail for a half mile to the left until reaching the AT. Turn left (south), and follow the AT nearly a mile back to Route 26. Cross the highway to the parking lot.

Special Note: For those looking for a more moderate climb to Table Rock (but skipping the slab caves), reverse the descent route, following the AT for a mile to the blue-blazed spur trail leading another half mile to Table Rock.

User Groups: Hikers only. Bikes and horses are prohibited; no wheelchair facilities. Dogs are discouraged along the Appalachian Trail in Maine. This trail would be difficult to snowshoe and is not suitable for skis.

Permits: Visitors using the parking lot at this trailhead are asked to pay a self-service fee of $2 per adult Maine resident/$3 per adult nonresident and $1 per child. There is a box beside the parking lot.

Maps: A very basic map of Grafton Notch State Park trails is available from park rangers, who are usually on duty at high-traffic areas such as Screw Auger Falls; it can also be obtained through the park office or the Maine Bureau of Parks and Lands. A detailed trail map is available from the Maine Appalachian Trail Club (Maine Highway 17 to Maine–New Hampshire State Line, $8). For a topographic area map, request Old Speck Mountain from the USGS.

Directions: This hike begins from a large parking lot (marked by a sign labeled Hiking Trail) where the Appalachian Trail crosses Route 26 in Grafton Notch State Park, 6.7 miles north of the sign at the state park's southern entrance and 1.8 miles south of the sign at the state park's northern entrance. Grafton Notch borders Route 26 between Upton and Newry. Grafton Notch State Park is open May 15–October 15, though the trails are accessible year-round.

GPS Coordinates: 44.6199 N, 70.9543 W

Contact: Grafton Notch State Park, 1941 Bear River Rd., Newry, ME 04261, 207/824-2912 or 207/624-6080 off-season. Maine Department of Conservation, Bureau of Parks and Lands, 286 Water St., Key Bank Plaza, 3rd and 5th floors, Augusta, ME 04333-0022, 207/287-3821, www.state.me.us/doc/parks. Maine Appalachian Trail Club, P.O. Box 283, Augusta, ME 04332-0283, www.matc.org.

12 MOTHER WALKER FALLS
0.2 mi/0.25 hr

in Grafton Notch State Park

Southeast of Grafton Notch, this short walk on an easy, wide path leads to viewpoints above Mother Walker Falls, an impressive gorge in the park cut by the erosive action of the Bear River.

From the turnout, walk down the stairs. A gravel path leads both to the right and to the left, and both directions lead a short distance to views into the narrow gorge, in which roaring water drops through several short steps for 100 yards or more. To the right, the walkway ends at a fence (and is a good choice if you have young kids in tow). If you go left, there is no fence, allowing greater liberty to explore the gorge. However, dense forest cover and rugged terrain here obscure any long views.

User Groups: Hikers and leashed dogs. This trail is not suitable for bikes or horses; no wheelchair facilities.

Permits: Parking and access are free.

Maps: Although no map is needed for this walk, a very basic map of Grafton Notch State Park trails is available from park rangers, who are usually on duty at Screw Auger Falls; it can also be obtained through the park office or the Maine Bureau of Parks and Lands. For a topographic area map, request Old Speck Mountain from the USGS.

Directions: This hike begins from a roadside turnout marked by a sign for Mother Walker Falls, on Route 26 in Grafton Notch State Park, 2.2 miles north of the sign at the state park's southern entrance and 6.3 miles south of the sign at the state park's northern entrance.

GPS Coordinates: 44.5814 N, 70.9253 W

Contact: Grafton Notch State Park, 1941 Bear River Rd., Newry, ME 04261, 207/824-2912 or 207/624-6080 off-season. Maine Department of Conservation, Bureau of Parks and Lands, 286 Water St., Key Bank Plaza, 3rd and 5th floors, Augusta, ME 04333-0022, 207/287-3821, www.state.me.us/doc/parks.

13 SCREW AUGER FALLS
0.1 mi/0.25 hr

in Grafton Notch State Park

BEST (

As the Bear River pours over smooth stone slabs, it tumbles through an impressive waterfall and a tight gorge of water-sculpted rock before stopping momentarily to form a pleasant pool of water. Sitting in the heart of 3,192-acre Grafton Notch State Park, Screw Auger Falls is a popular swimming hole for families and a scenic attraction for tourists. The gorge lies just a few minutes' stroll down a flat walkway from the parking lot. The short walk is well-marked and wheelchair-accessible.

User Groups: Hikers, wheelchair users, and leashed dogs. This trail is not suitable for bikes or horses.

Permits: Parking and access are free.

Maps: Although no map is needed for this walk, a very basic map of Grafton Notch State Park trails is available from park rangers, who are usually on duty at Screw Auger Falls; it can also be obtained through the park office or the state Bureau of Parks and Lands. For a topographic area map, request Old Speck Mountain from the USGS.

Directions: This hike begins from a large parking lot marked by a sign for Screw Auger Falls, on Route 26 in Grafton Notch State Park, one mile north of the sign at the state park's southern entrance and 7.5 miles south of the sign at the state park's northern entrance.

GPS Coordinates: 44.5832 N, 70.9031 W

Contact: Grafton Notch State Park, 1941 Bear River Rd., Newry, ME 04261, 207/824-2912 or 207/624-6080 off-season. Maine Department of Conservation, Bureau of Parks and Lands, 286 Water St., Key Bank Plaza, 3rd and 5th floors, Augusta, ME 04333-0022, 207/287-3821, www.state.me.us/doc/parks.

14 EYEBROW TRAIL
2.3 mi/1.5 hr

in Grafton Notch State Park

The Eyebrow Trail is a rugged side loop off the Appalachian Trail that offers a spectacular Grafton Notch view from the crest of Old Speck Mountain's towering cliffs, visible from the parking lot. Be forewarned: Parts of the trail are severely eroded and could be unpleasant, especially in wet weather. The elevation gain is about 1,000 feet.

From the parking lot, walk southbound on the white-blazed AT for about 100 yards and then bear right onto the orange-blazed Eyebrow Trail. The trail climbs very steeply over rugged terrain—at one point traversing an exposed slab of rock that could be dangerous when wet or icy. A bit more than a mile from the trailhead, the Eyebrow Trail passes over a series of four ledges. The view of Grafton Notch from the first ledge, a small overlook, is pretty good; the third ledge's view is largely obscured by trees. But from the second and fourth ledges you get an excellent, cliff-top view of Grafton Notch. The summit of Old Speck Mountain looms high to the right, Table Rock is distinguishable on the face of Baldpate Mountain directly across the notch, and Sunday River Whitecap rises prominently to the southeast. After enjoying the view, continue along the Eyebrow Trail 0.1 mile to its upper junction with the AT. Turn left and descend the AT for 1.1 miles back to the trailhead.

User Groups: Hikers only. Bikes and horses are prohibited; no wheelchair facilities. Dogs are discouraged along the Appalachian Trail in Maine. This trail should not be attempted in winter except by hikers experienced in mountaineering and prepared for severe winter weather, and is not suitable for skis.

Permits: Visitors using the parking lot at this trailhead are asked to pay a self-service fee of $2 per adult Maine resident/$3 per adult nonresident and $1 per child. There is a box beside the parking lot. The Old Speck summit

and northeast slopes are within Grafton Notch State Park in Maine.

Maps: Detailed trail maps are available from the Appalachian Mountain Club (Camden–Pleasant–Weld/Mahoosuc–Evans, $7.95 in waterproof Tyvek) and Maine Appalachian Trail Club (Maine Highway 17 to Maine–New Hampshire State Line, $8). For a topographic area map, request Old Speck Mountain from the USGS.

Directions: Park in the large parking lot located where the white-blazed Appalachian Trail crosses Route 26 (marked by a sign labeled Hiking Trail), 6.7 miles north of the sign at the state park's southern entrance and 1.8 miles south of the sign at the state park's northern entrance. Grafton Notch State Park is open May 15–October 15, though the trails are accessible year-round.

GPS Coordinates: 44.6385 N, 70.9566 W

Contact: Grafton Notch State Park, 1941 Bear River Rd., Newry, ME 04261, 207/824-2912 or 207/624-6080 off-season. Maine Department of Conservation, Bureau of Parks and Lands, 286 Water St., Key Bank Plaza, 3rd and 5th floors, Augusta, ME 04333-0022, 207/287-3821, www.state.me.us/doc/parks. Maine Appalachian Trail Club, P.O. Box 283, Augusta, ME 04332-0283, www.matc. org. Appalachian Mountain Club, 5 Joy St., Boston, MA 02108, 617/523-0655, www. outdoors.org.

15 STEP FALLS PRESERVE
1 mi/0.5 hr

south of Grafton Notch State Park, in Newry

BEST (

Step Falls is a steeply descending series of cascades and pools on the frothing white waters of Wight Brook. With a total drop of over 250 feet, it is one of the highest falls in Maine. A lodge and tourist cabins once stood in the area, advertising Step Falls as one of the most beautiful natural areas in western Maine. In 1909, the main lodge burned and the tourist operation disintegrated. Owned by the Nature Conservancy since 1962, forest cover has rebounded along Wight Brook, giving the falls a real sense of wild ruggedness.

From the parking lot, follow the obvious, white-blazed trail for a half mile along Wight Brook. (Considered a "braided brook" geologically, the Wight's rocky, foamy waters make an excellent environment for brook trout.) The trail is an easy, flat walk; take care not to wander off it onto false trails because such roaming tramples vegetation. Explore the base of the falls and head a bit further up to see the deep plunge pools formed by the action of ice and water splitting the underlying granite. Return the same way.

User Groups: Hikers and dogs. No bikes, horses, or wheelchair facilities.

Permits: Parking and access are free.

Maps: No map is needed for this easy walk. But for a topographic area map, request Old Speck Mountain from the USGS.

Directions: This hike begins from a large dirt parking lot off Route 26, 0.6 mile south of the Grafton Notch State Park southern entrance. Watch for a dirt road, marked by a small sign, on the south side of a small bridge over Wight Brook; it leads 100 feet to the parking area. The preserve is open dawn–dusk.

GPS Coordinates: 44.5695 N, 70.8714 W

Contact: The Nature Conservancy Maine Chapter, Fort Andross, 14 Maine St., Suite 401, Brunswick, ME 04011, www.nature. org.

16 OLD SPECK MOUNTAIN
7.6 mi/5 hr   𝄞4 ⛰7

in Grafton Notch State Park

This 7.6-mile round-trip hike brings you to the summit of Maine's fourth-highest peak and at a height of 4,180 feet, one of the state's 14 4,000-footers. Old Speck's summit lacked views until a fire tower was built there in 1999, replacing an old, unsafe tower. Now you can climb the tower for stunning, 360-degree views. There are also views along the Old Speck Trail, which coincides with the Appalachian Trail (AT), from the shoulder of Old Speck out over the vast sweep of woodlands to

© D TALBOT/WWW.GHOSTFLOWERS.COM

the view southeast across Mahoosuc Notch to the Northern Presidentials from the summit of Old Speck Mountain

the north. This hike's other attractions are the brook cascades, which the trail parallels lower on the mountain. The popular Grafton Notch hike climbs about 2,700 feet in elevation.

From the parking lot in Grafton Notch, follow the white blazes of the AT/Old Speck Trail southbound, following the playful waters of the dropping cascades. (The relaxing sound of falling water may help distract you from the steepness of the trail.) Leaving the brook behind by 1.5 miles, the trail continues relentlessly uphill. At 3.5 miles, reach a junction with the Mahoosuc Trail. Here, turn left on the Mahoosuc for the easy, final 0.3-mile climb to Old Speck's summit. Head back along the same route.

User Groups: Hikers only. Bikes and horses are prohibited; no wheelchair facilities. Dogs are discouraged along the Appalachian Trail in Maine. This trail should not be attempted in winter except by hikers experienced in mountaineering and prepared for severe winter weather, and is not suitable for skis.

Permits: Visitors using the parking lot at this trailhead are asked to pay a self-service fee of $3 per adult Maine resident/$2 per adult nonresident and $1 per child. There is a box beside the parking lot. The Old Speck summit and northeast slopes are within Grafton Notch State Park in Maine.

Maps: Detailed trail maps are available from the Appalachian Mountain Club (Camden–Pleasant–Weld/Mahoosuc–Evans, $7.95 in waterproof Tyvek) and the Maine Appalachian Trail Club (Maine Highway 17 to Maine–New Hampshire State Line, $8). For a topographic area map, request Old Speck Mountain from the USGS.

Directions: Grafton Notch State Park borders Route 26 between Upton and Newry. Park in the large parking lot located where the white-blazed Appalachian Trail crosses Route 26 (marked by a sign labeled Hiking Trail), 6.7 miles north of the sign at the state park's southern entrance and 1.8 miles south of the sign at the state park's northern entrance. Grafton Notch State Park is open May

15–October 15, though the trails are accessible year-round.

GPS Coordinates: 44.5901 N, 70.9443 W

Contact: Grafton Notch State Park, 1941 Bear River Rd., Newry, ME 04261, 207/824-2912 or 207/624-6080 off-season. Maine Department of Conservation, Bureau of Parks and Lands, 286 Water St., Key Bank Plaza, 3rd and 5th floors, Augusta, ME 04333-0022, 207/287-3821, www.state.me.us/doc/parks. Appalachian Mountain Club Pinkham Notch Visitor Center, P.O. Box 298, Gorham, NH 03581, 603/466-2721, www.outdoors.org. Maine Appalachian Trail Club, P.O. Box 283, Augusta, ME 04332-0283, www.matc.org.

17 MAHOOSUC NOTCH
6.5 mi/6 hr   👥5 ⛰10

south of Grafton Notch State Park

Strewn about on the floor of this deep, wild notch is a maze of stone and cavelike passages, formed by giant boulders which, over the eons, have fallen from the towering cliffs of Mahoosuc and Fulling Mill Mountains. Mahoosuc Notch can be hiked via the Notch Trail from Success Pond Road when the road is passable; it's 6.5 miles round-trip, climbs a cumulative 1,300 feet or so, and can easily take several hours; in many circles, the rocky obstacle course is known as one of the Appalachian Trail's most difficult miles. The shady notch is often much cooler than surrounding terrain; be sure to dress in layers, even in mid-summer.

From the Success Pond Road parking area, follow the Notch Trail as it ascends gently eastward through heavy cover of mixed forest. At 2.2 miles, it reaches a junction with the Mahoosuc Trail, which then coincides with the Appalachian Trail (AT). Bear left (northbound) on the AT, soon entering the boulder realm of the notch. Picking and crawling your way through the boulder field, carefully watch for white blazes to guide your next turn. Upon reaching the opposite end—you will know when you're through it—turn around and return the way you came, again watching for the white blazes.

For a two- or three-day loop that incorporates the notch and allows you to avoid backtracking through the notch, see *The Mahoosuc Range* hike in this chapter.

User Groups: Hikers only. Bikes and horses are prohibited; no wheelchair facilities. Dogs are discouraged along the Appalachian Trail in Maine.

Permits: Parking and access are free.

Maps: Detailed trail maps are available from the Appalachian Mountain Club (Camden–Pleasant–Weld/Mahoosuc–Evans, $7.95 in waterproof Tyvek) and the Maine Appalachian Trail Club (Maine Highway 17 to Maine–New Hampshire State Line, $8). For topographic area maps, request Success Pond and Old Speck Mountain from the USGS.

Directions: The Mahoosuc Notch Trail begins at a parking area off the dirt Success Pond Road, which runs south from Route 26, 2.8 miles north of where the white-blazed Appalachian Trail crosses the highway in Grafton Notch State Park. From Route 26, follow the twisting road for several miles, dipping over the state line and then back again to reach a left hand turn for the trailhead (look for the Notch Trail signpost). To access Success Pond Road from the south, drive north on Route 16 from its southern junction with U.S. 2 in Gorham, New Hampshire, for about 4.5 miles and turn east on the Cleveland Bridge across the Androscoggin River in Berlin, New Hampshire. Bear left onto Unity Street; go through the traffic light 0.7 mile from Route 16, and then continue 0.1 mile and bear right onto Hutchins Street. Drive 0.8 mile farther and turn sharply left, passing the paper company mill yard. Just 0.3 mile farther, turn right onto Success Pond Road. From Hutchins Street, it's about 11 miles to the trailhead parking area on the right at the Notch Trail sign. Success Pond Road, a private logging road that parallels the Mahoosuc Range on its west side, isn't

maintained in winter and may not be passable due to mud in spring.

GPS Coordinates: 44.5386 N, 71.0259 W

Contact: Appalachian Mountain Club Pinkham Notch Visitor Center, P.O. Box 298, Gorham, NH 03581, 603/466-2721, www.outdoors.org. Maine Appalachian Trail Club, P.O. Box 283, Augusta, ME 04332-0283, www.matc.org.

🔟🔢 THE MAHOOSUC RANGE

30.6 mi one-way/4-5 days

👥5 ⛰️10

between Shelburne, New Hampshire, and Grafton Notch State Park

BEST (

If you like the rugged adventure of a multi-day backpacking trek, you will love the journey offered by this wild, remote string of hills straddling the Maine–New Hampshire border; much of the route takes place on the Appalachian Trail (AT). Only one peak in the Mahoosucs—Old Speck—rises above 4,000 feet, but there's nary a flat piece of earth through the entire range. Read: Very tough hiking. Among the highlights are the ridge walk over Goose Eye Mountain, and Mahoosuc Notch, a boulder-strewn cleft in the range, often referred to as one of the most difficult miles on the Appalachian Trail. The route stretches from U.S. 2 in Shelburne, New Hampshire, to Grafton Notch, Maine, a 30.6-mile outing that can easily take five days. For a shorter trip, consider a two- or three-day hike from Grafton Notch to either the Mahoosuc Notch Trail (see the *Mahoosuc Notch* listing in this chapter) or the Carlo Col Trail.

The Centennial Trail, blazed in 1976 to commemorate the 100th anniversary of the Appalachian Mountain Club, is actually an old logging road and a shorter section of the Appalachian Trail. Leaving from the parking area, the familiar white blazes of the AT mark the Centennial Trailhead. Beginning on an old woods road, the Centennial Trail ascends steadily, and steeply at times, to the Mount Hayes eastern summit at 2.8 miles, which offers good views of the Carter–Moriah Range and the northern Presidentials to the south and southwest. At 3.1 miles, turn right (north) on the Mahoosuc Trail, which coincides with the white-blazed Appalachian Trail. (Just 0.2 mile to the left is a good view from the Mount Hayes summit.) At 4.9 miles, the AT passes over the open summit of Cascade Mountain and at 6.1 miles a side path leads 0.2 mile to the Trident Col campsite. The AT skirts Page Pond at 7.1 miles, and at 7.7 miles a side path leads to views from Wocket Ledge. At 8.8 miles, the trail runs along the north shore of Dream Lake; at the lake's far end, the Peabody Brook Trail diverges right, leading 3.1 miles south to North Road. (The Dryad Falls Trail branches east from the Peabody Brook Trail 0.1 mile from the AT and leads 1.8 miles to the Austin Brook Trail.) At 11 miles, the AT descends to Gentian Pond and a lean-to near its shore.

Continuing northbound, the trail climbs steeply up Mount Success, reaching the summit at 13.8 miles. After the Success Trail diverges left (west) at 14.4 miles (leading 2.4 miles to Success Pond Road), the AT descends steeply and then climbs to the Carlo Col Trail junction at 16.2 miles. (That trail leads 0.2 mile to the Carlo Col shelter and 2.6 miles west to Success Pond Road.) At 16.6 miles the AT passes over Mount Carlo's open summit, descends, and then climbs—very steeply near the top—to Goose Eye Mountain's high ridge at 18 miles. Walk the open ridge to the left a short distance for the terrific view from the west peak, where the Goose Eye Trail diverges left (west), leading 3.1 miles to Success Pond Road. Then turn north again on the AT, descend, and follow as it skirts the 3,794-foot east peak, around which the AT was rerouted in the 1990s because of damage by hikers to fragile alpine vegetation on its summit. (The two Wright Trail branches reach the AT immediately south and north of the east peak, both leading east about four miles to the Sunday River Ski Area road in Ketchum.) Descend again, climb over the summit of North Peak at 19.6 miles, and reach the Full Goose shelter at 20.6 miles. The AT climbs steeply north from the shelter to the barren South Peak summit, with views in nearly every direction. It swings left and then descends steeply to the junction with the Mahoosuc Notch Trail at 22.1 miles (the trail leads 2.2 miles west to Success Pond Road).

The next trail mile traverses the floor of Mahoosuc Notch, flanked by tall cliffs that usually leave the notch in cool shadow. Follow the white blazes carefully through the jumbled terrain of boulders, where carrying a backpack can be very difficult. At the notch's far end, at 23.1 miles, the AT swings uphill for the sustained climb of Mahoosuc Arm, passes ledges with good views, and then drops downhill to beautiful Speck Pond—at 3,430 feet, it's one of the highest ponds in Maine. There is a lean-to just above the pond's shore, at 25.7 miles; nearby, the Speck Pond Trail descends west 3.6 miles to Success Pond Road. From the shelter, the AT ascends north up Old Speck Mountain, traversing open ledges with excellent views to the south, then reentering the woods to reach a junction with the Old Speck Trail at 26.8 miles (where the Mahoosuc Trail ends). From that junction, the Old Speck Trail continues straight ahead 0.3 mile over easy ground to the 4,180-foot summit of Old Speck, where a fire tower offers glorious 360-degree views. The AT coincides with the Old Speck Trail for the circuitous, 3.5-mile descent to Grafton Notch, culminating at the parking lot.

Camping is permitted only at the five backcountry campsites along the Appalachian Trail through the Mahoosuc Range (Trident Col, Gentian Pond, Carlo Col, Full Goose, and Speck Pond). Backpackers stay in the shelters or use the tent platforms; all sites are free of charge except Speck Pond, which charges a caretaker fee of $8 per person per night. The Old Speck summit and northeast slopes are within Grafton Notch State Park in Maine, but the rest of the Mahoosucs are on private property and not a part of the White Mountain National Forest.

User Groups: Hikers only. Bikes and horses are prohibited; no wheelchair facilities. Dogs are discouraged along the Appalachian Trail in Maine. This trail should not be attempted in winter except by hikers experienced in mountaineering and prepared for severe winter weather.

Permits: Parking and access are free. All backcountry camping accommodations are free on a first-come, first-served basis, with the exception of Speck Pond. Campers at Speck Pond pay a cash-only caretaker fee of $8 per person, per night.

Maps: The best trail map for this route is the Camden–Pleasant–Weld/Mahoosuc–Evans map, $7.95 in waterproof Tyvek, available from Appalachian Mountain Club. The map available from the Main Appalachian Trail Club (Maine Highway 17 to Maine–New Hampshire State Line, $8) covers just the AT in Maine. For topographic area maps, request Berlin, Shelburne, Success Pond, Gilead, and Old Speck Mountain from the USGS.

Directions: You need to shuttle two vehicles for this backpacking trip. To hike the range from south to north, as described here, leave one vehicle in the large parking lot located where the white-blazed Appalachian Trail crosses Route 26 in Grafton Notch State Park (marked by a sign labeled Hiking Trail), 6.7 miles north of the sign at the state park's southern entrance and 1.8 miles south of the sign at the state park's northern entrance. To reach the start of this hike, turn north off U.S. 2 onto North Road in Shelburne, New Hampshire, about 3.2 miles east of the southern junction of U.S. 2 and Route 16 in Gorham. Cross the Androscoggin River, turn left onto Hogan Road, and continue 0.2 mile to a small parking area for the Centennial Trail.

GPS Coordinates: 44.5907 N, 70.9461 W

Contact: Grafton Notch State Park, 1941 Bear River Rd., Newry, ME 04261, 207/824-2912 or 207/624-6080 off-season. Maine Department of Conservation, Bureau of Parks and Lands, 286 Water St., Key Bank Plaza, 3rd and 5th floors, Augusta, ME 04333-0022, 207/287-3821, www.state.me.us/doc/parks. Appalachian Mountain Club Pinkham Notch Visitor Center, P.O. Box 298, Gorham, NH 03581, 603/466-2721, www.outdoors.org. Maine Appalachian Trail Club, P.O. Box 283, Augusta, ME 04332-0283, www.matc.org.

19 THE ROOST
1 mi/0.75 hr

in White Mountain National Forest, south of Gilead

Tucked away in the more remote Evans Notch is the Roost (1,374 ft.), a rocky outcropping above the Wild River with nice, though partially obscured, views west towards Mount Washington and Mount Clay. From the turnout, walk south across the bridge and turn left (east) on the Roost Trail. Cross two small brooks within the first quarter mile and then walk an old woods road. Less than a half mile from the trailhead, turn left (where indicated by an arrow and yellow blazes). Cross a brook and climb steeply uphill for the final 0.2 mile to the rocky knob of a summit; the views here are largely obstructed by trees. Follow the view sign and trail downhill for 0.1 mile to open ledges with a good view looking west over the Wild River Valley. This is a nice place to watch the sunset. Turn around and return the way you came. The elevation gain is about 500 feet.

User Groups: Hikers and dogs. This trail is not suitable for bikes or horses; no wheelchair facilities. Hunting is allowed in season. It is possible to ski and snowshoe this route; snow-covered trail conditions can be found here as early as late October and last some years through April, depending on weather conditions.

Permits: Parking and access are free.

Maps: For a contour map of trails, get the Map of Cold River Valley and Evans Notch, available from the Chatham Trails Association for $5, or the Appalachian Mountain Club's Carter Range–Evans Notch/North Country–Mahoosuc map ($7.95 in waterproof Tyvek). For a topographic area map, request Speckled Mountain from the USGS.

Directions: Drive to a turnout just north of the bridge over Evans Brook on Route 113, 3.7 miles south of the junction of Route 113 and U.S. 2 in Gilead and 7 miles north of where Route 113 crosses the Maine–New Hampshire border.

Route 113 through Evans Notch is not maintained in winter. In fact, gates are used to close off a 9.1-mile stretch of the highway. But you can drive to parking areas near the gates and ski or snowshoe the road beyond the gates to access this area. The northern gate on Route 113 is 1.6 miles south of the junction of U.S. 2 and Route 133 in Gilead. The southern gate sits on the Maine–New Hampshire line, 0.2 mile south of Brickett Place in North Chatham and immediately north of the White Mountain National Forest Basin Recreation Area entrance. The distance given for this hike is from the trailhead.

GPS Coordinates: 44.3592 N, 70.9847 W

Contact: Chatham Trails Association, 22 Grove Pl., Unit 29, Winchester, MA 01890, http://snebulos.mit.edu/orgs/cta. Appalachian Mountain Club Pinkham Notch Visitor Center, P.O. Box 298, Gorham, NH 03581, 603/466-2721, www.outdoors.org. White Mountain National Forest Supervisor, 719 North Main St., Laconia, NH 03246, 603/528-8721, TDD for the hearing impaired 603/528-8722, www.fs.fed.us/r9/white.

MOUNT CARIBOU
7.3 mi/4.5 hr   👥5 🏔9

in White Mountain National Forest, south of Gilead

This scenic 7.3-mile loop leads you past beautiful waterfalls and cascades to the top

of Mount Caribou, a hill with unusually excellent summit views for its 2,828-foot elevation. Caribou is part of the Caribou–Speckled Mountain Wilderness of the White Mountain National Forest. From this more isolated peak, take in a scenic vista that stretches north to the Androscoggin River Valley and south to the Speckled Mountain range peaks of Haystack, Butters, and Durgin Mountains. This loop gains more than 1,800 feet in elevation.

The Caribou Trail–Mud Brook Trail loop begins and ends at the parking area; this 7.3-mile hike follows it clockwise. Yellow blazes mark both trails only sporadically, though the paths are well used and obvious (except when covered with snow). Hike north (left from the parking area) on the Caribou Trail, crossing a wooden footbridge over a brook at 0.3 mile. About a half mile past the footbridge, the trail crosses Morrison Brook and trends in a more easterly direction—making several more stream crossings over the next two miles, some of which could be difficult at high water times. One stretch of about a half mile makes five crossings near several waterfalls and cascades, including 25-foot Kees Falls. Three miles from the trailhead, the Caribou Trail reaches a junction with the Mud Brook Trail, marked by a sign. Turn right (south) on the Mud Brook Trail and follow it a half mile, climbing steadily, to the open ledges of the summit. From various spots on the ledges you enjoy views of western Maine's low mountains and lakes in virtually every direction. Numerous false trails lead through the summit's scrub brush, so take care to follow cairns and faint yellow blazes over the summit, continuing on the Mud Brook Trail. A half mile below the summit, the trail traverses a cliff top with a good view east. From the summit, it's nearly four miles back to the parking area. Along its lower two miles, the trail parallels and twice crosses Mud Brook.

User Groups: Hikers and dogs. This trail is not suitable for bikes or horses; no wheelchair facilities. It is possible to ski and snowshoe this route; snow-covered trail conditions can be found here as early as late October and last some years through April, depending on weather conditions.

Permits: Parking and access are free.

Maps: For a contour map of trails, get the Map of Cold River Valley and Evans Notch for $5 from the Chatham Trails Association or the Carter Range–Evans Notch/North Country–Mahoosuc map, $7.95 in waterproof Tyvek, available from the Appalachian Mountain Club. For a topographic area map, request Speckled Mountain from the USGS.

Directions: The hike begins from a parking lot on Route 113, 4.8 miles south of its junction with U.S. 2 in Gilead and 5.9 miles north of where Route 113 crosses the Maine–New Hampshire border.

Route 113 through Evans Notch is not maintained in winter and gates are used to close off a 9.1-mile stretch of the highway. But you can drive to parking areas near the gates and ski or snowshoe the road beyond the gates to access this area. The northern gate on Route 113 is 1.6 miles south of the junction of U.S. 2 and Route 133 in Gilead. The southern gate sits on the Maine–New Hampshire line, 0.2 mile south of Brickett Place in North Chatham and immediately north of the White Mountain National Forest Basin Recreation Area entrance. The distance given for this hike is from the trailhead.

GPS Coordinates: 44.3470 N, 70.9803 W

Contact: Chatham Trails Association, 22 Grove Pl., Unit 29, Winchester, MA 01890, http://snebulos.mit.edu/orgs/cta. Appalachian Mountain Club Pinkham Notch Visitor Center, P.O. Box 298, Gorham, NH 03581, 603/466-2721, www.outdoors.org. White Mountain National Forest Supervisor, 719 North Main St., Laconia, NH 03246, 603/528-8721, TDD for the hearing impaired 603/528-8722, www.fs.fed.us/r9/white.

21 EAST ROYCE

3.0 mi/2 hr

in White Mountain National Forest, south of Gilead

Explore another small, rugged mountain overlooking the state line. The hike up East Royce (3,114 feet) makes several stream crossings, passing picturesque waterfalls and cascades, as it ascends the relentlessly steep mountainside. The uphill effort is worth it, though, as the East Royce summit offers sweeping views west to the dramatic cliffs of West Royce and the peaks of South and North Baldface in New Hampshire, and the lakes and lower hills of western Maine. The hike ascends about 1,700 feet.

From the parking lot, follow the East Royce Trail a steep 1.5 miles, crossing over, and then following, the cascading Evans Brook. Leaving the brook, the Royce Connector Trail enters from the left. Here, turn right to stay with the East Royce Trail, reaching open ledges that involve somewhat exposed scrambling within a quarter mile, and the summit just 0.1 mile farther. Return the way you came.

Special note: Across Route 113 from the parking area, the Spruce Hill Trail enters the woods beside a series of cascades worth checking out when the water is high.

User Groups: Hikers and dogs. This trail is not suitable for bikes or horses; no wheelchair facilities. It is possible to ski and snowshoe this route; snow-covered trail conditions can be found here as early as late October and last some years through April, depending on weather conditions.

Permits: Parking and access are free.

Maps: For a contour map of trails, get the Map of Cold River Valley and Evans Notch for $5 from the Chatham Trails Association or the Carter Range–Evans Notch/North Country–Mahoosuc map, $7.95 in waterproof Tyvek, from the Appalachian Mountain Club. For a topographic area map, request Speckled Mountain from the USGS.

Directions: The East Royce Trail begins at a parking lot on the west side of Route 113, 7.6 miles south of the junction of U.S. 2 and Route 113 in Gilead and 3.1 miles north of where Route 113 crosses the Maine–New Hampshire border.

Route 113 through Evans Notch is not maintained in winter, and gates are used to close off a 9.1-mile stretch of the highway. But you can drive to parking areas near the gates and ski or snowshoe the road beyond the gates to access this area. The northern gate on Route 113 is 1.6 miles south of the junction of U.S. 2 and Route 133 in Gilead. The southern gate sits on the Maine–New Hampshire line, 0.2 mile south of Brickett Place in North Chatham and immediately north of the White Mountain National Forest Basin Recreation Area entrance. The distance given for this hike is from the trailhead.

GPS Coordinates: 44.3104 N, 70.9865 W

Contact: Chatham Trails Association, 22 Grove Pl., Unit 29, Winchester, MA 01890, http://snebulos.mit.edu/orgs/cta. Appalachian Mountain Club Pinkham Notch Visitor Center, P.O. Box 298, Gorham, NH 03581, 603/466-2721, www.outdoors.org. White Mountain National Forest Supervisor, 719 North Main St., Laconia, NH 03246, 603/528-8721, TDD for the hearing impaired 603/528-8722, www.fs.fed.us/r9/white.

22 SPECKLED AND BLUEBERRY MOUNTAINS

7.9 mi/5 hr   👫5 ⛰9

in White Mountain National Forest, south of Gilead

From the bald, rocky crown of Speckled Mountain (2,906 ft.), the views are spectacular in almost every direction. But this hike is a twofer, taking you to the open ridge and ledges of Blueberry Mountain (1,781 ft.) and to a wide panorama of lakes and hills stretching to the south and east and back into Evans Notch. With a cumulative elevation gain of 2,400 feet, much of this hike, especially along the Blueberry Ridge Trail, makes for rugged a trip.

From the parking area, pick up the Bickford Brook Trail. At 0.6 mile, turn right at the sign for the Blueberry Ridge Trail. Immediately the trail makes a stream crossing at a narrow gorge that can be dangerous during high water. (If the stream is impassable or if you would prefer a less strenuous hike to the summit of Speckled Mountain, skip this trail and follow the Bickford Brook Trail all the way to the summit, an 8.6-mile round-trip.) Continue up the Blueberry Ridge Trail for 0.7 mile to a junction with the Lookout Loop, a half-mile detour out to the scenic ledges of the Blueberry Mountain cliffs. The Lookout Loop rejoins the Blueberry Ridge Trail; follow it to the right. It then ascends the two-mile ridge, much of it open, with wide views over your shoulder of the peaks across Evans Notch: East and West Royce, Meader, and North and South Baldface. At the upper junction with the Bickford Brook Trail, turn right (east) joining the trail for the easy half-mile hike to the Speckled summit. Descend via the Bickford Brook Trail all the way back (4.3 miles) to the parking area.

User Groups: Hikers and dogs. This trail is not suitable for bikes or horses; no wheelchair facilities. It is possible to ski and snowshoe this route; snow-covered trail conditions can be found here as early as late October and last some years through April, depending on weather conditions.

Permits: Parking and access are free.

Maps: For a contour map of trails, get the Map of Cold River Valley and Evans Notch for $5 from the Chatham Trails Association or the Carter Range–Evans Notch/North Country–Mahoosuc map, $7.95 in waterproof Tyvek, available from the Appalachian Mountain Club. For a topographic area map, request Speckled Mountain from the USGS.

Directions: This hike begins at Brickett Place, a parking area beside a brick building on

Route 113 in North Chatham, 0.2 mile north of where Route 113 crosses the Maine–New Hampshire border and 10.5 miles south of the junction of Route 113 and U.S. 2 in Gilead.

Route 113 through Evans Notch is not maintained in winter, and gates are used to close off a 9.1-mile stretch of the highway. But you can drive to parking areas near the gates and ski or snowshoe the road beyond the gates to access this area. The northern gate on Route 113 is 1.6 miles south of the junction of U.S. 2 and Route 133 in Gilead. The southern gate sits on the Maine–New Hampshire line, 0.2 mile south of Brickett Place in North Chatham and immediately north of the White Mountain National Forest Basin Recreation Area entrance. The distance given for this hike is from the trailhead.

GPS Coordinates: 44.2740 N, 71.0033 W

Contact: Chatham Trails Association, 22 Grove Pl., Unit 29, Winchester, MA 01890, http://snebulos.mit.edu/orgs/cta. Appalachian Mountain Club Pinkham Notch Visitor Center, P.O. Box 298, Gorham, NH 03581, 603/466-2721, www.outdoors.org. White Mountain National Forest Supervisor, 719 North Main St., Laconia, NH 03246, 603/528-8721, TDD for the hearing impaired 603/528-8722, www.fs.fed.us/r9/white.

23 SABATTUS MOUNTAIN
1.5 mi/1 hr   👫 2 ⛰ 9

outside Center Lovell

This short but popular local hike leads to the top of a sheer drop of hundreds of feet, providing wide views of nearly unbroken forest and mountains, including Pleasant Mountain to the south and the White Mountains to the east. This is a great hike for young children and fall foliage lovers. Follow the wide trail, which ascends steadily—and at times steeply—for 0.75 mile to the summit. Walk the cliff top to the right for the best views of the Whites. Return the same way.

User Groups: Hikers and dogs. This trail is not suitable for bikes or horses; no wheelchair facilities.

Permits: Parking and access are free.

Maps: No map is needed for this hike. The Camden–Pleasant–Weld/Mahoosuc–Evans map shows the location of Sabattus Mountain, but not its trail; the map is made of waterproof Tyvek and costs $7.95 from the Appalachian Mountain Club. For a topographic area map, request Center Lovell from the USGS.

Directions: From the Center Lovell Inn on Route 5 in Center Lovell, drive north for 0.2 mile on Route 5 and turn right on Sabattus Road. Continue for 1.5 miles and then bear right on the dirt Sabattus Mountain Road. Park in a small dirt lot or at the roadside 0.3 mile farther. The trail begins across the road from the lot.

GPS Coordinates: 44.1922 N, 70.8607 W

Contact: Maine Department of Conservation, Bureau of Parks and Lands, 286 Water St., Key Bank Plaza, 3rd and 5th floors, Augusta, ME 04333-0022, 207/287-3821, www.state.me.us/doc/parks.

24 JOCKEY CAP
0.4 mi/0.5 hr   👫 2 ⛰ 7

in Fryeburg

This short walk in Fryeburg—just down the road from North Conway, New Hampshire—leads to the top of what a sign along the trail describes as "the largest boulder in the United States." While that claim's veracity might be questionable, the hike does nonetheless provide a nice walk to a good view of the surrounding countryside, including Mounts Washington and Chocorua in the White Mountains.

Find the entrance gate to the Jockey Cap Trail between the Jockey Cap cabins and country store. Follow the wide and obvious trail into the woods. As the rocky face of Jockey Cap comes into view through the trees, the trail circles to the left around the boulder and emerges from the woods at a spot where you can safely walk up onto the cap. Return the same way.

User Groups: Hikers and dogs. No wheelchair facilities. This trail is not suitable for bikes, horses, or skis.

Permits: Parking and access are free.

Maps: No map is needed for this short walk, but for a topographic area map, request Fryeburg from the USGS.

Directions: From the junction of U.S. 302, Route 5, and Route 113 in Fryeburg, drive east on U.S. 302 for one mile and park at the Jockey Cap Country Store on the left. The Jockey Cap Trail begins at a gate between the store and the cabins to the right. The trail is open to the public year-round.

GPS Coordinates: 44.0216 N, 70.9622 W

Contact: This trail crosses private land owned by Quinn's Jockey Cap Country Store and Motel, 207/935-2306, www.quinnsjockeycap.com, and land owned by the town of Fryeburg and managed by its recreation department, 207/935-3933.

25 PLEASANT MOUNTAIN
5.7 mi/3.5 hr   🏃5 ⛰9

between Fryeburg, Denmark, and Bridgeton

Yes, it's a very pleasant trek to the top of Pleasant Mountain, one of the defining landmarks of the Sebago Lake region. Rising barely more than 2,000 feet above sea level, the mountain's ridge walk takes you through beautiful forest, over open ledges, and to several distinct summit humps, including excellent views from Big Bald Peak and Pleasant's main summit. This loop hike's cumulative elevation gain is about 1,600 feet.

From the turnout, pick up the Bald Peak Trail and begin a steady ascent beside a stream; watch for short waterfalls and a miniature flume. At 0.7 mile, the Sue's Way Trail and North Ridge Trail enter from the right, but stay left, climbing a steep 0.3 mile to Big Bald

Peak. From here, follow the Bald Peak Trail southward along the ridge, with excellent views. After 1.2 miles on the ridge, the Bald Peak Trail reaches a junction with the Fire Warden's Trail. Turn left here and proceed another 0.2 mile to the 2006-foot summit of Pleasant Mountain. Continue over the summit to pick up the Ledges Trail, which descends 1.8 miles along open ledges with terrific views to the south. The only downside to this descent route is found along the lower sections of this trail, which can be muddy and running with water. At the road, if you did not shuttle two vehicles, turn left and walk 1.5 miles to the Bald Peak Trailhead.

User Groups: Hikers and dogs. This trail is not suitable for bikes or horses; no wheelchair facilities.

Permits: Parking and access are free.

Maps: The area map Camden–Pleasant–Weld/Mahoosuc–Evans map, $7.95 in waterproof Tyvek, available from the Appalachian Mountain Club, shows this hike. The Loon Echo Land Trust offers a free, detailed map of trails in the Pleasant Mountain area, available for download on its website. For a topographic area map, request Pleasant Mountain from the USGS.

Directions: From the junction of U.S. 302 and Route 93, west of Bridgeton, drive 4.5 miles west on U.S. 302 and turn left onto Mountain Road (heading toward the Shawnee Peak Ski Area). Drive another 1.8 miles to a turnout at the Bald Peak Trailhead (marked by a sign on the right). If you have two vehicles, leave one at the Ledges Trailhead (marked by a sign) 1.5 miles farther down the road. Otherwise, you walk that stretch of road to finish this loop.

GPS Coordinates: 44.0457 N, 70.8032 W

Contact: Loon Echo Land Trust, 1 Chase St., Bridgton, ME 04009, 207/647-4352, www.loonecholandtrust.org. Appalachian Mountain Club, 5 Joy St., Boston, MA 02108, 617/523-0655, www.outdoors.org.

26 BURNT MEADOW MOUNTAIN
2.4 mi/2 hr 🥾3 ⛰7

outside Brownfield

A nice, short local hike, this hill near Brownfield has an open summit with views in almost every direction, from the White Mountains to the lakes of western Maine. Burnt Meadow was a ski area in the 1960s and 1970s and remnants of the ski operation can still be seen, though forest cover has all but completely taken back the bare slopes and runs that once stood here. Technically abandoned property that is opened to the public for recreational use, trails are maintained by volunteers from the Maine Appalachian Trail Club. This hike gains about 1,200 feet in elevation.

From the parking area, walk uphill to the old T-bar of a former ski area. Turn left and follow the T-bar and a worn footpath uphill. Ignore the sign with an arrow pointing to the right, which you encounter within the first half mile, and continue straight ahead under the T-bar. The trail grows quite steep, with lots of loose stones and dirt. Footing may become very tricky here in spring. Where the T-bar ends in a small clearing, turn left onto a trail marked by blue blazes, which leads at a more moderate angle to the summit. Watch for a good view from ledges on the left before reaching the summit. The broad top of Burnt Meadow Mountain offers views to the west, north, and south; continue over it and you get views to the south and east. Descend the way you came.

User Groups: Hikers and dogs. This trail is not suitable for bikes or horses; no wheelchair facilities.

Permits: Parking and access are free.

Maps: A trail map of Burnt Meadow Mountain can be found in the Maine Atlas, map 4 (Delorme Publishing). For a topographic area map, request Brownfield from the USGS.

Directions: From the junction of Route 5/113 and Route 160 in East Brownfield, turn west on Route 160 and continue 1.1 miles. Turn left, staying on Route 160, and continue another 0.3 mile. Turn right onto the paved Fire Lane 32 (shown as Ski Area Road on some maps). The parking area is 0.2 mile farther. The trailhead isn't marked, but there's an obvious parking area. The trail starts at the parking area's right side.

GPS Coordinates: 43.9361 N, 70.9038 W

Contact: Maine Appalachian Trail Club, P.O. Box 283, Augusta, ME 04332-0283, www.matc.org.

27 MOUNT CUTLER
2.6 mi/1.5 hr 🥾2 ⛰8

in Hiram

Rising abruptly from the floor of the Saco River Valley, Mount Cutler (1,232 ft.) is a short but rugged hike to views almost directly above the village of Hiram and west to the White Mountains. In its 1.3-mile route to the top, this hike climbs a steep 1,000 feet from the trailhead.

From the parking area, cross the railroad tracks, turn left, and then enter the woods on the right at a wide trail. Soon you branch right onto a red-blazed trail. The blazes appear sporadically at times, and on rocks rather than on trees higher up the mountain, making the trail potentially difficult to follow (particularly in winter). The trail ascends steep ledges overlooking the town of Hiram and grows narrow; care is needed over the ledges. But once you gain the ridge, the walking grows much easier as you pass through forests with a mix of hardwoods and hemlocks and traverse open areas with sweeping views. The east summit ledges, with views of the Saco Valley, are a good destination for a round-trip hike of about 1.5 miles. Continue on the trail along the ridge and into a saddle, where there's a birch tree grove. A faint footpath leads up the left side of the slope to the main summit, which is wooded. Just beyond it and to the right, however, is an open area with great views toward Pleasant Mountain and the White Mountains. Descend the way you came.

User Groups: Hikers and dogs. No wheelchair facilities. This trail is not suitable for bikes or horses.

Permits: Parking and access are free.

Maps: A trail map of Burnt Meadow Mountain can be found in the Maine Atlas, map 4 (Delorme Publishing). For topographic area maps, request Hiram and Cornish from the USGS.

Directions: From the junction of Route 117 and Route 5/113 in Hiram, drive over the concrete bridge; take an immediate left and then a right onto Mountain View Avenue. Drive about 0.1 mile and park at the roadside near the railroad tracks.

GPS Coordinates: 43.8778 N, 70.8052 W

Contact: Maine Appalachian Trail Club, P.O. Box 283, Augusta, ME 04332-0283, www.matc.org.

28 DOUGLAS HILL
1.2 mi/0.5 hr

south of Sebago

A short, scenic walk to the hill's open summit and its stone tower gives you expansive views of Sebago Lake, Pleasant Mountain, and the mountains to the northwest as far as Mount Washington. This 169-acre preserve, formerly owned by The Nature Conservancy, is now owned by the town of Sebago.

From the registration box, walk through the stone pillars, follow the yellow-blazed Woods Trail a short distance, and then bear left onto the Ledges Trail (also blazed yellow). This trail leads over interesting open ledges with good views, though they are slick when wet. At the summit, climb the stone tower's steps; on top is a diagram identifying the distant peaks. A nature trail, blazed orange, makes a 0.75-mile loop off the summit and returns to it. Descend back to the parking lot via the

Woods Trail, which is a more direct descent than the Ledges Trail.

User Groups: Hikers only. No wheelchair facilities. This trail is not suitable for bikes or horses and is not open in winter. Dogs are prohibited.

Permits: Parking and access are free; just register at the trailhead.

Maps: A free guide and map to Douglas Hill is available at the trailhead registration box. For topographic area maps, request Steep Falls and North Sebago from the USGS.

Directions: From the junction of Routes 107 and Macks Corner Road in East Sebago, drive a half mile north on Route 107 and turn left onto Douglas Hill Road (which is one mile south of Sebago center). On some maps, the road is not labeled. Drive 0.8 mile to a hilltop and take a sharp left. In another half mile, turn left into a small parking area. The preserve is open only during daylight hours.

GPS Coordinates: 43.8741 N, 70.6985 W

Contact: Sebago Town Hall, 406 Bridgton Rd., Sebago, ME 04029, 207/787-8884.

29 WOLFE'S NECK WOODS
2 mi/1 hr

in Freeport

A five minute drive from Freeport's busy shopping district, the marshes, forests, and open fields of Wolfe's Neck State Park are a welcome pocket of calm in the midst of what can be a very crowded tourist city. (Plus, it's a great place to try out some of that hiking gear you just loaded up on at L.L.Bean.) This flat loop of approximately two miles winds through the Wolfe's Neck Woods, taking you to many of the park's best features, including a white pine forest, salt marshes, and the rocky shorelines of Casco Bay and the Harraseeket River estuary. The White Pine Trail portion of this hike is wheelchair accessible.

From the parking area, pick up the White Pine Trail, a level, universally accessible trail that leads deep into a tall forest of pine and hemlock. Meandering a bit at first, the trail reaches the marshy shore of Casco Bay within 0.2 mile. Interpretive panels explain sites along the trail, including information about the park's signature resident: the osprey. Nearby Googins Island (just offshore and clearly visible from the trail) is a popular northern nesting ground for the graceful bird. Dozens can be seen summering on the island; bring binoculars for the best views of young osprey taking flight for perhaps the very first time. The Casco Bay Trail, a footpath, continues on past the island overlook; those who wish to stay on the universally accessible path can turn right to return to the parking area (The White Pine Trail loop is approximately 0.4 mile long). Following the shores of the bay for another 0.3 mile, the trail turns inland and becomes the Harraseeket River Trail. In less than a half mile, the trail brings you to the shores of the Harraseeket River. Hugging the shoreline for approximately 0.2 mile, the trail offers nice views west toward Freeport. Turning inland again, follow the trail another 0.3 mile back to the parking area.

User Groups: Hikers, leashed dogs, and wheelchairs. No bikes or horses.

Permits: Visitors to Wolfe's Neck Woods pay $3 per adult Maine resident/$4.50 per adult nonresident and $1.50 per child May–October. Trails are still open in the off-season.

Maps: A trail map and informational brochure is available at the trailhead. For a topographic area map, request Freeport from the USGS.

Directions: From downtown Freeport, drive 4.5 miles east on Route 1 to a right turn at Bow Street. Follow a short distance to Wolfe Neck Road and the park entrance.

GPS Coordinates: 43.8217 N, 70.0840 W

Contact: Wolfe's Neck Woods State Park, 426 Wolfe's Neck Rd., Freeport, ME 04032, 207/865-4465. Maine Department of Conservation, Bureau of Parks and Lands, 286 Water St., Key Bank Plaza, 3rd and 5th floors, Augusta, ME 04333-0022, 207/287-3821, www.state.me.us/doc/parks.

30 PORTLAND: BACK COVE TRAIL AND EASTERN PROMENADE

3.1 mi/1.5 hr

in Portland

BEST (

Portland is consistently rated as one of the healthiest places to live in the United States, and you'll see why as you join dozens of Portlanders for a walk or jog along the Back Cove Trail. Just off I-295, and not far from Portland's bustling city center, this wheelchair-accessible loop circles the beautiful shores of Back Cove and is an urban oasis for jogging, biking, and just strolling along taking in great views of the city skyline. The trail is a combination of stone dust and paved surfaces— mostly flat with a slight rise along the stretch that parallels I-295. And with its numerous benches along the trail and portable toilets available near both parking areas, it's a great place to bring kids. The loop is a popular recreation area for Portland locals—especially for early morning and late afternoon joggers.

Access the trail from either of the two parking lots—in Payson Park on the north end of the loop or from the Preble Street Extension on the south shore of Back Cove. A good route for views is to leave from Payson Park, bearing right on the trail (counterclockwise). On your left, for the first mile or so, is the Portland city skyline, a mix of old brick buildings and gleaming modern structures. Continuing to skirt the southern and eastern shores of the cove, views look over the pleasant water, eventually looping back to reach Payson Park.

Special Note: Before returning to Payson Park, the trail crosses a bridge over the watery entrance to Back Cove. On the southern end of the bridge, another wheelchair-accessible trail leads to the right. This is Eastern Promenade Trail, a two-mile loop along Casco Bay. The waterfront trail, part of an old rail line, offers spectacular harbor and ocean views. Approximately one mile from leaving Back Cove, the "Eastern Prom" reaches East End

Beach and Fort Allen Park. The trail loops back from Fort Allen Park and eventually rejoins the main Eastern Prom for the return to Back Cove. The trailhead can also be accessed at the corner of Commercial and India Streets. To reach the East End Beach parking area, descend from Fort Allen Park down Cutter Street to the parking area.

User Groups: Hikers, leashed dogs, bikes, and wheelchairs. No horses.

Permits: Access and parking are free.

Maps: Trail maps of both Back Cove and the Eastern Promenade are available from Portland Trails. For topographic area maps, request Portland East and Portland West from the USGS.

Directions: To reach Payson Park and the parking area off Preble Street: From the intersection of Marginal Way and Forest Avenue/U.S. 302 in Portland, turn onto U.S. 302, heading west under I-293. After passing the highway exit ramps, take the first right onto Baxter Boulevard/Route 1 North. Follow 1.7 miles to

a right turn at Preble Street. The parking area is at the end of the street to the right.

GPS Coordinates: 43.6790 N, 70.2681 W

Contact: Portland Trails, 305 Commercial St., Portland, ME, 04101, 207/775.2411, www.trails.org.

31 MOUNT AGAMENTICUS
1 mi/0.75 hr   👣2 ⛰7

west of Ogunquit

BEST (

Mount Agamenticus (known locally as Mount A) is famous as one of Maine's best sites for hawk-watching. Each fall, thousands of migrating hawks, including peregrine falcons, bald eagles, osprey, and northern goshawks, can be viewed from the summit. On an early October day with strong northwest winds, hundreds of raptors may soar over the mountain in just a few hours. This one-mile hike up and

On Mount Agamenticus, an interpretive panel identifies the far-off peaks of the White Mountains, including Mount Washington.

down tiny Agamenticus (689 ft.) is an easy walk to a summit with a fire tower and two viewing platforms that offer 360-degree views of the Seacoast region and southern Maine and New Hampshire.

From the parking area at the base of Summit Road, follow the Ring Trail, an old woods road. Reaching a fork within 0.1 mile of the trailhead, bear left, crossing over Summit Road and soon reaching another junction. Here, turn right on the Blueberry Bluff Trail and continue uphill to the broad summit area. Mount A's summit is grassy and broad with two viewing platforms, a town recreation lodge, and fire tower; despite all this development, there's still plenty of room to picnic and just roam about. The only mar to this beautiful place is the very large (and very out of place) cell tower. Return the way you came or descend via Summit Road.

User Groups: Hikers and dogs. Parts of the trail are not suitable for bikes or horses. Refer to the map found at the trailhead for trails on the mountain open to biking and horseback riding. No wheelchair facilities on the trail. Summit Road leads to a level parking area with wheelchair access.

Permits: Parking and access are free.

Maps: A trail map and informational brochure is available at the trailhead. For topographic area maps, request York Harbor and North Berwick from the USGS.

Directions: From the corner of U.S. 1 and York Street in York, drive north on U.S. 1 for 4.1 miles to a left turn on Mountain Road. Follow 2.6 miles to a right turn on Summit Road (listed as the Mount A Road on some maps). Park in the turnouts at the base of the road. GPS Coordinates: 43.2169 N, 70.6922 W

Contact: York Parks and Recreation Department, 186 York St., York, ME 03909, 207/363-1040, www.parksandrec.yorkmaine.org. The Nature Conservancy Maine Chapter, Fort Andross, 14 Maine St., Suite 401, Brunswick, ME 04011, 207/729-5181, www.nature.org. The Nature Conservancy Southern Maine Field Office, 207/646-1788.

32 VAUGHAN WOODS
2 mi/1 hr

in South Berwick

A few miles east of Kittery and only a half mile from the village center of South Berwick, Vaughan Woods is a lush forest of pine and hemlock running for nearly one mile along the banks of the placid Salmon River. Seemingly oblivious to the development of the past century, trails in the area take you through stands of giant trees more than a hundred years old and to views of the historic Hamilton House, an 18th century mansion that was once the centerpiece of bustling farmlands.

From the parking area, walk towards the bathroom and leave on the River Run Trail. Heading downhill a short distance, the trail is immediately surrounded by soaring pines. Following a rocky stream dropping off to the left, the trail reaches the river within 0.1 mile. Bear left to stay on the River Run Trail, stepping carefully over exposed tree roots. Benches at scenic overlooks along the trail invite you to stop and gaze for a few moments at the bucolic beauty of the Salmon River, a tidal tributary of the Piscataqua River estuary. Across the water is the rural town of Rollinsford, New Hampshire, and in keeping with Vaughan's lost-in-time feel, all that's visible on the other shore is ancient farmland that's still in active use; on quiet days, you may even hear the mooing of a grazing dairy herd.

After a mile, the trail ends at the Bridle Path. Turn left and head uphill through the woods, passing the old Warren homesite, now marked with a plaque for one of the area's first inhabitants. Continue on the Bridle Path for the next mile back to the park area and enjoy the quiet solitude of the woods.

User Groups: Hikers, leashed dogs, and horses. No bikes or on-trail wheelchair facilities (the bathroom and picnic area are wheelchair accessible).

Permits: At the payment box at the entrance to the park, visitors pay a self-service fee of $2 per adult Maine resident/$3 per adult nonresident and $1 per child.

Maps: A trail map and informational brochure is available at the trailhead. For a topographic area map, request Dover East from the USGS.

Directions: From the intersection of Routes 4 and 236 in South Berwick, drive south on Route 236 for approximately a half mile. Turn right opposite the junior high school at Vine Street. Go about one mile to the intersection of Vine Street and Old Fields Road. Turn right and watch for the park entrance on the right.

GPS Coordinates: 43.2116 N, 70.8088 W

Contact: Vaughan Woods State Park, 28 Oldsfields Rd., South Berwick, ME 03908, 207/490-4079. Maine Department of Conservation, Bureau of Parks and Lands, 286 Water St., Key Bank Plaza, 3rd and 5th floors, Augusta, ME 04333-0022, 207/287-3821, www.state.me.us/doc/parks.

Index

A–B

Acadia Mountain: 68
Acadia Traverse: 70
Barren Mountain and Slugundy Gorge: 52
Beech and Canada Cliffs: 67
Beech Mountain: 66
Bernard and Mansell Mountains: 69
Bigelow Mountain: 92
Bigelow Range: 91
Borestone Mountain: 53
Burnt Meadow Mountain: 116

C–D

Cadillac Mountain: South Ridge Trail: 81
Cadillac Mountain: West Face Trail: 73
Cobscook Bay State Park: 84
Dorr and Cadillac Mountains: 71
Doubletop Mountain: 42
Douglas Hill: 117

E–H

East Royce: 112
Eyebrow Trail: 105
Flying Mountain: 69
Gorham Mountain: 82
Great Head: 75
Great Wass Island: 83
Gulf Hagas: 51
Half a 100-Mile Wilderness: 49
Hamlin Peak: 32

I–K

Isle au Haut: Duck Harbor Mountain/Merchant Point Loop: 63
Isle au Haut: Eben's Head: 61
Isle au Haut: Western Head Loop: 64
Jockey Cap: 114
Jordan Pond Loop: 80

Jordan Pond/Eagle Lake/Bubble Pond Carriage Road Loop: 72
Jordan Pond/Sargent Mountain Carriage Road Loop: 78
Katahdin Stream Falls: 38
Katahdin: Abol Trail: 36
Katahdin: Hunt Trail: 37
Katahdin: Knife Edge Loop: 33
Katahdin: Saddle Trail: 35
Kidney Pond Loop: 43

L–M

Little Abol Falls: 37
Mahoosuc Notch: 107
Maiden Cliff: 59
Mother Walker Falls: 104
Mount Abraham: 95
Mount Agamenticus: 119
Mount Caribou: 111
Mount Coe: 41
Mount Cutler: 116
Mount Megunticook Traverse: 59
Mount O-J-I: 42

N–P

North Brother: 40
North Traveler Mountain: 27
Ocean Lookout: 60
Ocean Path: 77
Old Blue Mountain: 101
Old Speck Mountain: 106
100-Mile Wilderness: 45
Pemetic Mountain: 81
Penobscot and Sargent Mountains: 77
Piazza Rock and the Caves: 100
Pleasant Mountain: 115
Pollywog Gorge: 44
Portland: Back Cove Trail and Eastern Promenade: 118

Q–S

Quoddy Head State Park: 85
Russell Pond/Davis Pond Loop: 30
Sabattus Mountain: 114
Saddleback Mountain and The Horn: 99
Saddleback Range: 97
Sandy Stream Pond/Whidden Ponds Loop: 32
Screw Auger Falls: 104
South Branch Falls: 27
South Turner Mountain: 31
Spaulding Mountain: 95
Speckled and Blueberry Mountains: 113
Step Falls Preserve: 105
Sugarloaf Mountain: 94

T–Z

Table Rock, Grafton Notch: 103
The Beehive: 76
The Bubbles/Eagle Lake Loop: 74
The Mahoosuc Range: 108
The Owl: 39
The Roost: 110
Traveler Loop: 28
Tumbledown Mountain Brook Trail: 102
Vaughan Woods: 120
White Cap Mountain: 50
Wolfe's Neck Woods: 117

www.moon.com

DESTINATIONS | ACTIVITIES | BLOGS | MAPS | BOOKS

MOON.COM is ready to help plan your next trip! Filled with fresh trip ideas and strategies, author interviews, informative travel blogs, a detailed map library, and descriptions of all the Moon guidebooks, Moon.com is all you need to get out and explore the world—or even places in your own backyard. While at Moon.com, sign up for our monthly e-newsletter for updates on new releases, travel tips, and expert advice from our on-the-go Moon authors. As always, when you travel with Moon, expect an experience that is uncommon and truly unique.

MOON IS ON FACEBOOK—BECOME A FAN!
JOIN THE MOON PHOTO GROUP ON FLICKR

"Well written, thoroughly researched, and packed full of useful information and advice, these guides really do get you into the outdoors."

—GORP.COM

MOON MAINE HIKING

Avalon Travel
a member of the Perseus Books Group
1700 Fourth Street
Berkeley, CA 94710, USA
www.moon.com

Editor: Elizabeth Hollis Hansen
Series Manager: Sabrina Young
Copy Editor: Naomi Adler Dancis
Graphics and Production Coordinator:
   Domini Dragoone
Cover Designer: Domini Dragoone
Interior Designer: Darren Alessi
Map Editor: Mike Morgenfeld
Cartographers: Mike Morgenfeld, Kat Bennett
Proofreader: Nikki Ioakimedes

ISBN-13: 978-1-59880-562-8

Text © 2010 by Avalon Travel and Jacqueline
Tourville.
Maps © 2010 by Avalon Travel.
All rights reserved.

Front cover photo: Hikers enjoying ocean view in
   Acadia © Lmphot | Dreamstime.com
Title page photo: A resting bench offers nice
   views of the Salmon Falls River in Vaughan
   Woods State Park © J. D. Brown

Printed in the United States of America

ABOUT THE AUTHOR

Jacqueline Tourville

Jacqueline Tourville grew up hiking in the Adirondacks region of New York State. As an adult, she discovered the diverse terrain of New England while living in Boston. Today, she's a busy freelance writer and author of the popular "Are We There Yet?" family travel column for *Parenting New Hampshire* magazine. She is the co-author of the prenatal health guide *Big, Beautiful and Pregnant,* and has contributed numerous articles about health and outdoor living for both web and print publications. Jacqueline lives in New Hampshire with her husband and two children.